DICTIONARY OF
ENGLISH USAGE

DICTIONARY OF ENGLISH USAGE

BETTY KIRKPATRICK

Bloomsbury Books
London

This edition published 1995 by Bloomsbury Books,
an imprint of Godfrey Cave Associates,
42 Bloomsbury Street, London, WC1B 3QJ.

ISBN 1 85471 525 9

Printed in UK

A

a *and* **an** are the forms of the indefinite article. The form **a** is used before words that begin with a consonant sound, as in *a* box, *a* garden, *a* road, *a* wall. The form **an** is used before words that begin with a vowel sound, as in *an* apple, *an* easel, *an* ostrich, *an* uncle. Note that it is the *sound* of the initial letter that matters and not the *spelling*. Thus **a** is used before words beginning with a *u* when they are pronounced with a *y* sound as though it were a consonant, as *a* unit, *a* usual occurrence. Similarly **an** is used, for example, before words beginning with the letter *h* where this is not pronounced, as in *an* heir, *an* hour, *an* honest man.

Formerly it was quite common to use **an** before words that begin with an *h* sound and also begin with an unstressed syllable, as in *an* hotel (ho-*tel*), *an* historic (his-*tor*-ik) occasion, *an* hereditary (her-*ed*-it-ary) disease. It is more usual nowadays to use **a** in such cases, ignoring the question of the unstressed syllable.

abbreviations are shortened forms of words, usually used as a space-saving technique and are becoming increasingly common in modern usage. They frequently take the form of the initial letters of several words as, for example, in the title of an organization, person, etc, e.g.

TUC (Trade Union Council) or BBC (British Broadcasting Corporation), JP (Justice of the Peace). Note that, unlike acronyms, abbreviations are not pronounced as words even when this would be possible. Thus TUC is not pronounced *tuk*.

Abbreviations may also be formed from the first and last letters of a word (when they are known as contractions), e.g. Dr (Doctor), Rd (Road), St (Street or Saint), pd (paid). Many of these are found mainly in written, rather than spoken, form.

Abbreviations may also be formed from the first few letters of a word, e.g. Feb (February), Prof (Professor), Rev (Reverend).

In modern usage the tendency is to omit full stops from abbreviations. This is most true of abbreviations involving initial capital letters, as in TUC, BBC, EEC and USA. In such cases full stops should definitely not be used if one or some of the initial letters do not belong to a full word. Thus 'television' is abbreviated to TV.

There are usually no full stops in abbreviations involving the first and last letters of a word (contractions), as in Dr, Mr, Rd, St, but this is a matter of taste.

Abbreviations involving the first few letters of a word, as in Prof for 'Professor', are the most likely to have full stops, as Feb. for 'February', but again this is now a matter of taste.

Plurals in abbreviations are mostly formed by adding lower-case *s*, as in Drs, JPs, TVs. Note the absence of apostrophes.

See also **acronyms**.

abdomen is now usually pronounced with the emphasis on the first syllable (*ab*-do-men).

aberration is frequently misspelt. Note the single *b* and double *r*. It means deviation or departure from what is considered normal, as in 'mental aberration'.

-able *and* **-ible** are both used to form adjectives. It is easy to confuse the spelling of words ending in these, and the best way to get them right is to memorize them, unless you have a good knowledge of Latin. Words ending in **-ible** are usually formed from Latin words ending in *-ibilis*, and some words ending in **-able** are formed from Latin words ending in *-abilis*.

In addition, some words ending in **-able** are derived from French, and words formed from English words end in **-able** rather than **-ible**. The form **-able** is what is known as a 'living suffix' and is the form that is used when coining modern words, as 'a sackable offence', 'washable materials', 'a jailable crime', 'a kickable ball', 'a catchable ball'.

Some words ending in **-able**:

abominable	healable	manageable	sizeable
acceptable	hearable	measurable	solvable
agreeable	identifiable	memorable	stoppable
bearable	impeccable	nameable	storable
beatable	immutable	nonflammable	tenable
blameable	impracticable	objectionable	tolerable
comfortable	inapplicable	operable	touchable
commendable	inappreciable	palpable	undoable
delectable	incalculable	passable	usable
discreditable	indispensable	purchasable	variable

-abled

disreputable	indescribable	rateable	viable
enviable	indisputable	readable	washable
forgettable	lamentable	reviewable	wearable
forgivable	laudable	saleable	winnable
governable	likeable	shakeable	workable

Some words ending in **-ible**:

accessible	discernible	indelible	repressible
admissible	divisible	intelligible	reproducible
audible	edible	irascible	resistible
collapsible	exhaustible	legible	responsible
combustible	expressible	negligible	reversible
compatible	fallible	ostensible	risible
comprehensible	feasible	perceptible	sensible
contemptible	flexible	permissible	susceptible
credible	forcible	plausible	tangible
defensible	gullible	possible	visible
digestible			

-abled is a suffix meaning 'able-bodied'. It is most usually found in such phrases as 'differently abled', a 'politically correct', more positive way of referring to people with some form of disability, as in 'provide access to the club building for differently abled members'. In common with many politically correct terms, it is disliked by many people, including many disabled people.

ableism *or* **ablism** means discrimination in favour of able-bodied people as in 'people in wheelchairs unable to get jobs because of ableism'. Also known as **able-bodiedism** and **able-bodism**. Note that the suffix '-ism' is often used to indicate discrimination against the group to which it refers, as in 'ageism'.

Aboriginal rather than **Aborigine** is now the preferred term for an original inhabitant of Australia, especially where the word is in the singular.

abscess, meaning an inflamed swelling with pus in it, is frequently misspelt. Note the *c* after the first *s*.

abuse *and* **misuse** both mean wrong or improper use or treatment. However, **abuse** tends to be a more condemnatory term, suggesting that the wrong use or treatment is morally wrong or illegal. Thus we find 'misuse of the equipment' or 'misuse of one's talents', but 'abuse of a privileged position' or 'abuse of children'. 'Child abuse' is usually used to indicate physical violence or sexual assault.

Abuse is also frequently applied to the use of substances that are dangerous or injurious to health, as 'drug abuse', 'solvent abuse', or 'alcohol abuse'. In addition, it is used to describe insulting or offensive language, as in 'shout abuse at the referee'.

academic is used to describe scholarly or educational matters, as 'a child with academic rather than sporting interests'. From this use it has come to mean theoretical rather than actual or practical, as in 'wasting time discussing matters of purely academic concern'. In modern use it is frequently used to mean irrelevant, as in 'Whether you vote for him or not is academic. He is certain of a majority of votes'.

accelerate, meaning 'to go faster', is a common word that is frequently misspelt. Note the double *c* but single *l*.

accent commonly refers to a regional or individual way of speaking or pronouncing words, as in 'a Glasgow accent'. The word is also used to mean emphasis, as in 'In hotel the accent is on the second syllable of the word', or 'In fashion this year the accent is no longer on shirts'.

Accent also refers to certain symbols used on some foreign words adopted into English. In modern usage, which has a tendency to punctuate less than was formerly the case, accents are frequently omitted. For example, an actor's part in a play is now usually spelt 'role' but originally it was spelt 'rôle', the accent on *o* being called a circumflex. The accent is most likely to be retained if it affects the pronunciation. Thus 'cliché' and 'divorcé' usually retain the acute accent, as it is called, on the *e*. On the other hand, the accent known as the cedilla is frequently omitted from beneath the *c* in words such as 'façade/facade', although it is there to indicate that the *c* is soft, pronounced like an *s*, rather than a hard sound pronounced like a *k*.

access is commonly misspelt. Note the double *c* and double *s*. The word is usually a noun meaning 'entry or admission', as in 'try to gain access to the building', or 'the opportunity to use something', as in 'have access to confidential information'. It is also used to refer to the right of a parent to spend time with his or her children, as in 'Father was allowed access to the children at weekends'.

However **access** can also be used as a verb. It is most commonly found in computing, meaning obtaining information from, as in 'accessing details from the computer file relating to the accounts'. In modern usage many technical words become used, and indeed overused, in the general language. Thus the verb **access** can now be found meaning to obtain information not on a computer, as in 'access the information in the filing cabinet'. It can also be found in the sense of gaining entry to a building, as in 'Their attempts to access the building at night were unsuccessful'.

accessory and **accessary** are interchangeable as regards only one meaning of **accessory**. A person who helps another person to commit a crime is known either as an **accessory** or an **accessary**, although the former is the more modern term. However, only **accessory** is used to describe a useful or decorative extra that is not strictly necessary, as in 'Seat covers are accessories that are included in the price of the car' and 'She wore a red dress with black accessories' ('accessories' in the second example being handbag, shoes and gloves).

accompany can be followed either by the preposition 'with' or 'by'. When it means 'to go somewhere with someone', 'by' is used, as in 'She was accompanied by her parents to church' Similarly, 'by' is used when **accompany** is used in a musical context, as in 'The singer was accompanied on the piano by her brother'. When **accompany** means 'to go along with something' or 'supplement something', either 'by' or 'with' may be used, as in 'The roast turkey was accompanied by all the trimmings', 'His words were accompanied by/with a gesture of dismissal', and 'The speaker accompanied his words with expressive gestures'.

accommodation is one of the most commonly misspelt words. Note the double *c*, and double *m*.

acetic is a common misspelling of **ascetic** although it is a

11

word in its own right. **Acetic** refers to the acid used in vinegar and is used to mean sour. **Ascetic** means 'self-denying' or 'self-disciplined' and is used to refer to a person (or to his/her lifestyle) who abstains from many of life's pleasures and who is often a recluse. A person who has such a lifestyle is known as an **ascetic.**

acknowledgement and **acknowledgment** are both accept-able spellings.

acoustics can take either a singular or plural verb. When it is being thought of as a branch of science it is treated as being singular, as in 'Acoustics deals with the study of sound', but when it is used to describe the qualities of a hall, etc, with regard to its sound-carrying properties, it is treated as being plural, as in 'The acoustics in the school hall are very poor'.

acquaint is often misspelt. It is a common error to omit the *c*. It means 'to become familiar with' or 'to inform'. The same problem arises in the word **acquaintance**, which means 'someone whom one knows slightly'.

acquire, acquirement and **acquisition** are all frequently misspelt. It is a common error to omit the *c*.

acronyms, like some **abbreviations,** are formed from the initial letters of several words. Unlike **abbreviations,** however, **acronyms** are pronounced as words rather than as just a series of letters. For example OPEC (Organiza-tion of Petroleum Producing Countries) is pronounced *o*-pek and is thus an acronym, unlike USA (United States of America) which is pronounced as a series of letters and *not* as a word (*oo*-sa or *yoo*-sa) and is thus an **ab-breviation.**

Acronyms are written without full stops, as in UNESCO (United Nations Educational, Scientific and Cultural Organization). Mostly **acronyms** are written in capital letters, as in NASA (National Aeronautics and Space Administration). However, very common **acronyms,** such as Aids (Acquired Immune Deficiency Syndrome), are written with just an initial capital, the rest of the letters being lower case.

Acronyms that refer to a piece of scientific or technical equipment are written like ordinary words in lowercase letters, as 'laser' (light amplification by simulated emission of radiation).

A fashion originated in the mid 1980s for inventing **acronyms** relating to lifestyles or categories of society. These included 'yuppie', also spelt 'yuppy', which is an acronym of 'young urban (or upwardly mobile) professional'. 'Yuppie' became an established part of the language, as to a certain extent did 'nimby' (not in my back yard), an **acronym** that indicates people's reluctance to have any new developments, such as a hostel for ex-prisoners, in the vicinity of their homes, even if they are in theory in general favour of such developments. The majority of **acronyms** coined at this time were short-lived and are no longer commonly used. These included 'dinky' ('dual or double income, no kids') and 'woopie' ('well-off older person'). The fashion in forming such acronyms became rather silly, resulting in such words as 'pippie' ('person inheriting parents' property') and 'whanny' ('we have a nanny').

acrylic refers to the fibre used in a kind of man-made textile. The word is commonly misspelt. Note the *y*, not *i*, before the *l*.

activate and **actuate** both mean 'make active' but are commonly used in different senses. **Activate** refers to physical or chemical action, as in 'The terrorists activated the explosive device'. **Actuate** means 'to move to action' and 'to serve as a motive', as in 'The murderer was actuated by jealousy'.

acute and **chronic** both refer to disease. **Acute** is used of a disease that is sudden in onset and lasts a relatively short time, as in 'Flu is an acute illness'. **Chronic** is used of a disease that may be slow to develop and lasts a long time, possibly over several years, as in 'Asthma is a chronic condition'.

acumen is now usually pronounced *ak*-yoo-men, with the emphasis on the first syllable, although formerly the stress was usually on the second syllable (yoo). It means 'the ability to make good or shrewd judgements, as in 'a woman of excellent business acumen'.

actress is still widely used as a term for a woman who acts in plays or films, although many people prefer the term 'actor', regarding this as a neutral term rather than simply the masculine form. The **-ess** suffix, used to indicate the feminine form of a word, is generally becoming less common as these forms are regarded as sexist or belittling. *See also* **-ess**.

AD and **BC** are abbreviations that accompany year numbers. **AD** stands for 'Anno Domini', meaning 'in the year of our Lord' and indicates that the year concerned is one occurring after Jesus Christ was born. Traditionally **AD**

is placed before the year number concerned, as in 'Their great-grandfather was born in AD 1801', but in modern usage it sometimes follows the year number, as in 'The house was built in 1780 AD.' **BC** stands for 'Before Christ' and indicates that the year concerned is one occurring before Jesus Christ was born. It follows the year number, as in 'The event took place in Rome in 55 BC'.

adagio is a musical direction indicating that a piece or passage of music should be played slowly. It is an Italian word meaning 'at ease' and is pronounced a-*dah*-jee-o.

adapter and **adaptor** can be used interchangeably, but commonly **adapter** is used to refer to a person who adapts, as in 'the adapter of the stage play for television and **adaptor** is used to refer to a thing that adapts, specifically a type of electrical plug.

ad hoc is a Latin phrase commonly used in English to mean 'for a particular purpose only', as in 'An ad hoc committee was formed to deal with the flooding of the town'.

adjourn is commonly misspelt. Note the *d* before the *j*. It means either 'to postpone or stop for a short time', as in 'The meeting will adjourn for lunch', and 'to go', as in 'They adjourned to another room'.

admissible is frequently misspelt. Note the -IBLE ending.

admission and **admittance** both mean 'permission or right to enter'. **Admission** is the more common term, as in 'They refused him admission to their house', and, unlike **admittance**, it can also mean 'the price or fee charged for entry' as in 'Admission to the football match

15

is £3'. **Admittance** is largely used in formal or official
situations, as in 'They ignored the notice saying "No
Admittance" '. **Admission** also means 'confession' or
'acknowledgement of responsibility', as in 'On her own
admission she was the thief'.

admit may be followed either by the preposition 'to' or
the preposition 'of', depending on the sense. In the sense
of 'to confess', **admit** is usually not followed by a preposition at all, as in 'He admitted his mistake' and 'She
admitted stealing the brooch'. However, in this sense
admit is sometimes followed by 'to', as in 'They have
admitted to their error' and 'They have admitted to their
part in the theft'.

In the sense of 'to allow to enter', **admit** is followed
by 'to', as in 'The doorman admitted the guest to the
club'. Also in the rather formal sense of 'give access or
entrance to', **admit** is followed by 'to', as in 'the rear
door admits straight to the garden'. In the sense of 'to be
open to' or 'leave room for', **admit** is followed by 'of',
as in 'The situation admits of no other explanation'.

admittance *see* **admission**.

adolescence is frequently misspelt. Note the letters *sc* in
the middle of the word. Adolescence refers to the period
of life between puberty and adulthood.

adopted and **adoptive** are liable to be confused. **Adopted**
is applied to children who have been adopted, as in 'The
couple have two adopted daughters'. **Adoptive** is applied to a person or people who adopt a child, as in 'Her
biological parents tried to get the girl back from her adoptive parents'.

adult may be pronounced with the emphasis on either of the two syllables. Thus *a*-dult and a-*dult* are both acceptable although the pronunciation with the emphasis on the first syllable (*a*-dult) is the more common. The adjective **adult** means 'mature', as in 'a very adult young man' and 'for adults' as in 'courses in adult education'. However it can also mean 'pornographic', as in 'adult movies'.

adversary is commonly pronounced with the emphasis on the first syllable (*ad*-ver-sar-i) although in modern usage it is also found with the emphasis on the second syllable (ad-*ver*-sar-i).

adverse and **averse** are often confused because they sound and look rather alike, although they are different in meaning. **Adverse** means 'unfavourable' or 'hostile', as in 'Her actions had an adverse effect on her career' and 'The committee's proposals met with an adverse reaction'. **Averse** means 'unwilling' or 'having a dislike', as in 'The staff are not averse to the reconstruction plans', 'Her mother is totally averse to her marrying him'. Note that **averse** is followed by the preposition 'to'.

   Adverse is usually pronounced with the emphasis on the first syllable (*ad*-vers) and **averse** is always pronounced with the emphasis on the second syllable (a-*vers*).

advertise is commonly misspelt. It is not one of those verbs that can end in either -*ise* or -*ize*. 'Advertize' is an erroneous spelling.

advice and **advise** are sometimes confused. **Advice** is a noun meaning 'helpful information or guidance', as in

17

adviser

'She asked her sister's advice on clothes' and 'She should seek legal advice'. **Advise** is a verb meaning 'to give advice', as in 'The career's office will advise you about educational qualifications'. It can also mean to 'inform', as in 'The officer advised the men of the change of plan'. It is usually used in a formal or official context. Note that it is wrong to spell advise with a *z*.

adviser and **advisor** are both acceptable spellings. The word is applied to someone who gives advice, usually someone in a professional or official capacity, as in 'He is a financial adviser/advisor'.

aerial is commonly misspelt. Note the *ae* at the beginning of the word. **Aerial** as an adjective means either 'of the air', as in 'aerial changes', or 'from the air or an aircraft', as in 'an aerial view'.

aeroplane is commonly abbreviated to **plane** in modern usage. In American English **aeroplane** becomes **airplane.**

affect and **effect** are often confused. **Affect** is a verb meaning 'to have an effect on', 'to influence or change in some way', as in 'His health was affected by his poor working conditions', 'Their decision was affected by personal prejudice'. It is often confused with **effect,** a noun meaning 'result or consequence' or 'influence', as in 'Their terrible experiences will have an effect on the children'. **Effect** is also a verb used mostly in formal contexts and means 'to bring about', as in 'The company plans to effect major changes'. **Affect** can also mean 'to pretend or feign' as in 'She affected an appearance of poverty although she was very wealthy'.

affinity may be followed by the preposition 'with' or 'between', and means 'close relationship', 'mutual attraction' or similarity, as in 'the affinity which twins have with each other' and 'There was an affinity between the two families who had lost children'. In modern usage it is sometimes followed by 'for' or 'towards', and means 'liking', as in 'She has an affinity for fair-haired men'.

aficionado is frequently misspelt. Note the single *f* and single *n*. It means a fan or supporter as in 'an aficionado of jazz', 'an opera aficionado', and is pronounced a-fiss-eon-*ah*-do. The plural is **aficionados**.

afters *see* **dessert**.

aged has two possible pronunciations depending on the sense. When it means 'very old', as in 'aged men with white beards', it is pronounced *ay*-jid. When it means 'years of age', as in 'a girl aged nine', it is pronounced with one syllable, *ayjd*.

ageing in modern usage may also be spelt **aging.**

ageism means discrimination on the grounds of age, as in 'By giving an age range in their job advert the firm were guilty of ageism'. Usually it refers to discrimination against older or elderly people, but it also refers to discrimination against young people.

agenda in modern usage is a singular noun having the plural **agendas**. It means 'a list of things to be attended to', as in 'The financial situation was the first item on the committee's agenda'. Originally it was a plural noun, derived from Latin, meaning 'things to be done'.

aggravate literally means 'to make worse', as in 'Her remarks simply aggravated the situation'. In modern usage it is frequently found meaning 'to irritate or annoy', as in 'The children were aggravating their mother when she was trying to read'. It is often labelled as 'informal' in dictionaries and is best avoided in formal situations.

agnostic and **atheist** are both words meaning 'disbeliever in God', but there are differences in sense between the two words. **Agnostics** believe that it is not possible to know whether God exists or not. **Atheists** believe that there is no God.

agoraphobia is frequently misspelt. Note the *o*, not *a*, after *g*. The word means 'fear of open spaces'.

alcohol abuse is a modern term for alcoholism. *See* **abuse**.

alibi is derived from the Latin word for 'elsewhere'. It is used to refer to a legal plea that a person accused or under suspicion was somewhere other than the scene of the crime at the time the crime was committed. In modern usage **alibi** is frequently used to mean simply 'excuse' or 'pretext', as in 'He had the perfect alibi for not going to the party—he was ill in hospital'.

align is frequently misspelt. Note the single *l*. The word means either 'to bring into (a straight) line', as in 'align the wheels of a car', or 'to support, be on the side of', as in 'He aligned himself with the rebels'.

all right is frequently misspelt as 'alright'. Although 'alright' is commonly found, it is still regarded as an error.

allude should be used only in the meaning of 'to refer indirectly to', as in 'When he spoke of people who had suffered from mental illness he was alluding to himself'. It should not be used simply to mean 'to refer to', as in 'In his speech he alluded frequently to the fact that he

was retiring', although this is commonly found nowadays in informal contexts.

allusion and **illusion** are liable to be confused because of
the similarity in their pronunciation, but they are completely different in meaning. **Allusion** means 'an indirect reference', as in 'His remarks on poverty in the area
were an allusion to the hardship of his own childhood
there'. *See* **allude**. **Illusion** means 'a false or misleading
impression', as in 'Putting a screen round her part of the
room gave at least the illusion of privacy'.

alternate and **alternative** are liable to be confused. **Alternate** means 'every other' or 'occurring by turns', as
in 'They visit her mother on alternate weekends' and
'between alternate layers of meat and cheese sauce'.
Alternative means 'offering a choice' or 'being an alternative', as in 'If the motorway is busy there is an alternative route'. **Alternative** is found in some cases in
modern usage to mean 'not conventional, not traditional', as in 'alternative medicine' and 'alternative come-
dy'.

   Alternative as a noun refers to the choice between two
possibilities, as in 'The alternatives are to go by train or
by plane'. In modern usage, however, it is becoming
common to use it to refer also to the choice among two
or more possibilities, as in 'He has to use a college from
five alternatives'.

although and **though** are largely interchangeable but
though is slightly less formal, as in 'We arrived on time
although/though we left late'.

all together and **altogether** are not interchangeable. **All**

together means 'at the same time' or 'in the same place', as in 'The guests arrived all together' and 'They kept their personal papers all together in a filing cabinet'. **Altogether** means 'in all, in total' or 'completely', as in "We collected £500 altogether' and 'The work was altogether too much for him'.

a.m. and **p.m.** are liable to be confused. **A.M.**, which is short for Latin 'ante meridiem' meaning 'before noon', is used to indicate that the time given occurs between the hours of midnight and midday, as in 'She asked friends for coffee at 11 a.m'. **P.M.**, which is short for *post meridiem*, meaning 'after noon', is used to indicate that the time given occurs during the hours between midday and midnight, as in 'The shop stays open until 10 p.m.' Full stops are usually used both in **a.m.** and **p.m.**; in the case of **a.m.** to distinguish it from the verb 'am'. Usually both **a.m.** and **p.m.** are spelt with lower-case letters.

amend and **emend** are liable to be confused. Both words mean 'to correct', but **emend** has a more restricted use than **amend**. **Emend** means specifically 'to remove errors from something written or printed', as in 'The editor in the publishing office emended the author's manuscript'. **Amend** means 'to correct', 'to improve' or 'to alter', as in 'We have overcharged you but we shall amend the error', and 'The rules for entry are old-fashioned and have to be amended'.

amiable and **amicable** both refer to friendliness and goodwill. **Amiable** means 'friendly' or 'agreeable and pleasant', and is mostly used of people or their moods, as in 'amiable neighbours', 'amiable travelling companions', 'of an amiable temperament' and 'be in an amiable mood'. **Amicable** means 'characterized by friendliness and goodwill' and is applied mainly to relationships, agreements, documents, etc, as in 'an amicable working relationship', 'reach an amicable settlement at the end of the war' and 'send an amicable letter to his former rival'.

among and **amongst** are interchangeable, as in 'We searched among/amongst the bushes for the ball,' 'Divide the chocolate among/amongst you', and 'You must choose among/amongst the various possibilities'.

among and **between** may be used interchangeably in most contexts. Formerly **between** was used only when referring to the relationship of two things, as in 'Share the chocolate between you and your brother', and **among** was used when referring to the relationship of three or more things, as in 'Share the chocolate among all your friends'. In modern usage **between** may be used when referring to more than two things, as in 'There is agreement between all the countries of the EC' and 'Share the chocolate between all of you'. However, **among** is still used only to describe more than two things.

amoral and **immoral** are not interchangeable. **Amoral** means 'lacking moral standards, devoid of moral sense', indicating that the person so described has no concern with morals, as in 'The child was completely amoral and did not know the difference between right and wrong'. **Immoral** means 'against or breaking moral standards, bad'. 'He knows he's doing wrong but he goes on being

an

completely immoral' and 'commit immoral acts'. Note
the spelling of both words. **Amoral** has only one *m* but
immoral has double *m*.

an *see* **a**.

anaesthetic and **analgesic** are liable to be confused. As
an adjective, **anaesthetic** means 'producing a loss of
feeling', as in 'inject the patient with an anaesthetic substance', and as a noun it means 'a substance that produces a loss of feeling', as in 'administer an anaesthetic
to the patient on the operating table'. A local anaesthetic
produces a loss of feeling in only part of the body, as in
'remove the rotten tooth under local anaesthetic'. A **general anaesthetic** produces loss of feeling in the whole
body and induces unconsciousness, as in 'The operation
on his leg will have to be performed under general anaesthetic'. As an adjective **analgesic** means 'producing
a lack of or reduction in, sensitivity to pain, pain-kill-
ing', as in 'aspirin has an analgesic effect'. As a noun
analgesic means 'a substance that produces a lack of, or
reduction in, sensitivity to pain', as in 'aspirin, paraceta-
mol, and other analgesics'.

analyse is frequently misspelt. Note that it is not one of
those verbs that can end in -*ize*. However, in American
English 'analyze' is the accepted spelling.

annex and **annexe** are not interchangeable. Annex is a
verb meaning 'to take possession of', as in 'The enemy
invaders annexed the country' or 'to add or attach', as in
'She annexed a note to the document'. **Annexe** is a noun
meaning 'a building added to, or used as an addition to,
another building', as in 'build an annexe to the house as

a workshop' and 'some school classes taking place in an annexe'.

antihistamine is sometimes misspelt. Note the *i*, not *y*, after *h*. **Antihistamine** is used to treat allergies.

apostrophe is a form of punctuation that is mainly used to indicate possession. Many spelling errors centre on the position of the apostrophe in relation to *s*.

Possessive nouns are usually formed by adding *'s* to the singular noun, as in 'the girl's mother', and Peter's car'; by adding an apostrophe to plural nouns that end in *s*, as in 'all the teachers' cars'; by adding *'s* to irregular plural nouns that do not end in *s*, as in 'women's shoes'.

In the possessive form of a name or singular noun that ends in *s*, *x* or *z*, the apostrophe may or may not be followed by *s*. In words of one syllable the final *s* is usually added, as in 'James's house', 'the fox's lair', 'Roz's dress'. The final *s* is most frequently omitted in names, particularly in names of three or more syllables, as in 'Euripides' plays'. In many cases the presence or absence of final *s* is a matter of convention.

The apostrophe is also used to indicate omitted letters in contracted forms of words, as in 'can't' and 'you've'. They are sometimes used to indicate missing century numbers in dates, as in 'the '60s and '70s', but are not used at the end of decades, etc, as in '1960s', not '1960's'.

Generally apostrophes are no longer used to indicate omitted letters in shortened forms that are in common use, as in 'phone' and 'flu'.

Apostrophes are often omitted wrongly in modern usage, particularly in the media and by advertisers, as in

appal

'womens hairdressers', 'childrens helpings'. In addition, apostrophes are frequently added erroneously (as in 'potato's for sale' and 'Beware of the dog's'). This is partly because people are unsure about when and when not to use them and partly because of a modern tendency to punctuate as little as possible.

appal is very frequently misspelt. Note the double *p* and single *l*. Note also the double *ll* in **appalled** and **appalling**.

arbiter and **arbitrator**, although similar in meaning, are not totally interchangeable. **Arbiter** means 'a person who has absolute power to judge or make decisions', as in 'Parisian designers used to be total arbiters of fashion'. **Arbitrator** is 'a person appointed to settle differences in a dispute', as in 'act as arbitrator between management and workers in the wages dispute'. **Arbiter** is occasionally used with the latter meaning also.

archaeology is liable to be misspelt. Note the order of the three vowels in the middle—*aeo*.

artist and **artiste** are liable to be confused. **Artist** refers to 'a person who paints or draws,' as in 'Renoir was a great artist'. The word may also refer to 'a person who is skilled in something', as in 'The mechanic is a real artist with an engine'. **Artiste** refers to 'an entertainer, such as a singer or a dancer', as in 'a list of the artistes in the musical performances'. The word is becoming a little old-fashioned.

asphyxiate is frequently misspelt. Note that it has *y*, not *i*, before *x*. It means 'to suffocate', as in 'asphyxiate his victim with a pillow'.

assassinate is frequently misspelt. Note the two sets of double *s*. It means 'to murder, especially someone of political importance', as in 'Rebels assassinated the president'. Note also the spelling of **assassin**, 'a person who assassinates someone'.

asthma is frequently misspelt. Note the *th*, which is frequently wrongly omitted. The word refers to 'a chronic breathing disorder'.

atheist *see* **agnostic.**

at this moment in time is an overused phrase meaning simply 'now'. In modern usage there is a tendency to use what are thought to be grander-sounding alternatives for simple words. It is best to avoid such overworked phrases and use the simpler form.

au fait is French in origin but it is commonly used in English to mean 'familiar with' or 'informed about', as in 'not completely au fait with the new office system'. It is pronounced *o* fay.

aural and **oral** are liable to be confused because they sound similar and are both related to parts of the body. **Aural** means 'of the ear' or 'referring to the sense of hearing', as in 'aural faculties affected by the explosion' and 'The children were given an aural comprehension test (that is, one that one was read out to them) in French'. **Oral** means 'of the mouth' or 'referring to speech', as in 'oral hygiene' and 'an oral examination' (that is, one in which questions and answers are spoken, not written).

aurally challenged means 'deaf' or 'hard of hearing'. It is part of the 'politically correct' movement to make a personal problem or disadvantage appear in a positive

authoress

rather than a negative light. Although the intention behind it is a good one, the phrase, and others like it, have not really caught on, and such phrases are indeed subject to ridicule because they sound rather high-flown.

authoress is not used in modern usage since it is considered sexist. **Author** is regarded as a neutral term to describe both male and female authors.

averse *see* **adverse**.

avoid *see* **evade**.

avoidance *see* **evasion**.

B

bachelor is frequently misspelt, it being common, and wrong, to include a *t* before the *c*. Note that the term **bachelor girl** is objected to by many women for the same reason that they object to adding *-ess* to the masculine to make a feminine form, as in 'authoress'.

backward and **backwards** in British English are respectively adjective and adverb. Examples of **backward** include 'take a backward step' and 'The child is rather backward for his age'. Examples of **backwards** include 'take a step backwards'. In American English **backward** is frequently used as a adverb.

bacteria is a plural noun, the singular form being **bacterium**, which is found mainly in scientific or medical texts. Thus it is correct to say 'a stomach infection caused by bacteria in the water' but quite wrong to say 'an infection caused by a bacteria'.

bail and **bale** are liable to be confused. **Bail** as a noun means 'the security money deposited as a guarantee that an arrested person will appear in court', as in 'Her family provided money for her bail' and 'Her brother stood bail for her.' It also has a verb form, as in 'His friends did not have enough money to bail him'. This verb often takes the form **bail out**. **Bale** is a noun meaning 'a bundle', as in 'a bundle of hay'.

baited

    Bail and **bale** are both acceptable forms of the verb meaning 'to scoop', as in 'The fishermen had to bail/bale water out of the bottom of the boat'. Similarly, both forms of the verb are acceptable when they mean 'to make an emergency parachute jump from a plane', as in 'The plane caught fire and the pilot had to bail/bale out'.

baited *see* **bated.**

bale *see* **bail.**

balk and **baulk** are both acceptable spellings of the verb meaning 'to refuse or be reluctant to do something', as in 'She balked/baulked at paying such a high price for a dress' and 'to obstruct or prevent', as in 'She was balked/baulked in her attempt at swimming the Channel by bad weather'.

banal is frequently mispronounced. It should rhyme with 'canal', with the emphasis on the second syllable (ba-*nal*).

banister, meaning 'the handrail supported by posts fixed at the side of a staircase', may be spelt **bannister** but it is a less common form.

barmaid is disliked by many people on the grounds that it sounds a belittling term and is thus sexist. It is also disliked by people who are interested in political correctness. However the word continues to be quite common, along with **barman**, and efforts to insist on **bar assistant** or **barperson** have not yet succeeded.

basis, meaning 'something on which something is founded', as in 'The cost of the project was the basis of his argument against it', has the plural form **bases** although it is not commonly used. It would be more usual to say 'arguments without a firm basis' than 'arguments without firm bases'.

basically means literally 'referring to a base or basis, fundamentally', as in 'The scientist's theory is basically unsound', but it is frequently used almost meaninglessly as a fill-up word at the beginning of a sentence, as in 'Basically he just wants more money'. Overuse of this word should be avoided.

bated, as in 'with bated breath' meaning 'tense and anxious with excitement', is frequently misspelt **baited**. Care should be taken not to confuse the two words.

bath and **bathe** are not interchangeable. **Bath** as a verb means 'to have a bath', as in 'He baths every morning' or 'to wash someone in a bath', as in 'The mother bathed the baby in a small tin bath'. **Bathe**, on the other hand, is used to mean 'to wash (a wound, etc)', as in 'She bathed the boy's grazed knee with warm water' or 'to swim in the sea', as in 'too cold to bathe today'. In American English **bathe** is used in the sense of 'have a bath', as in 'prefer to bathe than take a shower'.

bathroom *see* **toilet**.

baulk *see* **balk**.

BC *see* AD.

beat and **beaten** are frequently used wrongly. **Beat** is the past tense of the verb 'to beat', as in 'Our team beat the opposition easily' and 'His father used to beat him when he was a child'. **Beaten** is the past participle of the verb 'to beat', as in 'We should have beaten them easily' and 'He thought the child should have been beaten for his bad behaviour'.

beautiful

beautiful is frequently misspelt. Note the order of the vowels (*eau*). Note also the single *l*.

because means 'for the reason that', as in 'He left because he was bored', and is sometimes misused. It is wrong to use it in a sentence that also contains 'the reason that', as in 'The reason she doesn't say much is that she is shy'. The correct form of this is 'She doesn't say much because she is shy' or 'The reason she doesn't say much is that she is shy'.

because of *see* **due to**.

beg the question is often used wrongly. It means 'to take for granted the very point that has to be proved', as in 'To say that God must exist because we can see all his wonderful creations in the world around us begs the question'. The statement assumes that these creations have been made by God although this has not been proved and yet this fact is being used as evidence that there is a God. **Beg the question** is often used wrongly to mean 'to evade the question', as in 'The police tried to get him to say where he had been but he begged the question and changed the subject'.

beige, meaning 'a pale brown colour', is frequently misspelt. Note the order of *e* and *i*. The pronunciation of the word may also cause difficulties. It is pronounced *bayzh*.

benefit causes problems with the parts of the verb. The past tense is **benefited**, as in 'They benefited from having had an excellent education'. The present participle is **benefiting**, as in 'Benefiting from the will of their late uncle they were able to buy a bigger house'. Note the single *t*.

benign means 'kindly, well-disposed' when applied to people, as in 'fortunate enough to have a benign ruler'. This meaning may also be used of things, as in 'give a benign smile' and 'live in a benign climate'. As a medical term **benign** means 'nonmalignant, non-cancerous'. **Innocent** is another word for **benign** in this sense.

beside and **besides** are not interchangeable. **Beside** is a preposition meaning 'by the side of', as in 'The little girl wants to sit beside her friend' and 'They walked beside each other all the way'. **Beside** is also found in the phrase **'beside oneself'**, meaning 'extremely agitated', as in 'The children were beside themselves with excitement waiting to go on a picnic' and 'He was beside himself with rage when his rival won the prize'.

Besides has several meanings. It means 'moreover, in addition', as in 'The house is overpriced. Besides, it's too far from the village'. It also means 'as well as, in addition to', as in 'We have visited many countries besides France', and 'other than, except for', as in 'They are interested in nothing besides work' and 'I have told no one besides you'.

bet is the common form of the past tense and past participle of the verb 'to bet', as in 'He bet me he could run faster than me' and 'He would have bet hundreds of pounds that the horse he fancied would win'. 'Placed a bet' is an alternative form, as in 'He has never placed a bet in his life' as an alternative to 'He has never bet in his life'. The form **betted** exists but it is rare.

bête noire refers to 'something that one detests or fears', as in 'Loud pop music is her father's bête noire, although

33

betted

she sings with a pop group'. Note the spelling, particularly the accent (circumflex) on **bête** and the *e* at the end of **noire.** The phrase is French in origin and the plural form is **bêtes noires,** as in 'A bearded man is one of her many bêtes noires'.

betted *see* **bet.**

better should be preceded by 'had' when it means 'ought to' or 'should', as in 'You had better leave now if you want to arrive there by nightfall' and 'We had better apologize for upsetting her'. In informal contexts, especially in informal speech as in 'Hey Joe, Mum says you better come now', the 'had' is often omitted but it should be retained in formal contexts. The negative form is 'had better not', as in 'He had better not try to deceive her'.

between *see* **among.**

between is often found in the phrase 'between you and me' as in 'Between you and me I think he stole the money'. Note that 'me' is correct and that 'I' is wrong. This is because prepositions like 'between' are followed by an object, not a subject. 'I' acts as the subject of a sentence, as in 'I know her', and 'me' as the object, as in 'She knows me'.

bi- Of the words beginning with the prefix **bi-,** biannual and biennial are liable to be confused. **Biannual** means 'twice a year' and **biennial** means 'every two years'.

Bicentenary and **bicentennial** both mean 'a 200th anniversary', as in 'celebrating the bicentenary/bicentennial of the firm'. **Bicentenary** is, however, the more common expression in British English, although **bicentennial** is more common in American English.

Biweekly is a confusing word as it has two different meanings. It means both 'twice a week' and 'once every two weeks'. Thus there is no means of knowing without other information whether 'a bi-weekly publication' comes out once a week or every two weeks. The confusion arises because the prefix 'bi-', which means 'two', can refer both to doubling, as in 'bicycle', and halving, as in 'bisection'.

biannual *see* **bi-**.

bias should become **biased** and **biasing** in the past tense and past participle, and the present participle, respectively, as in 'The behaviour of some of the competitors biased the judges against them' and in 'The behaviour of some of the competitors seem to be biasing the judges against them.'. However in modern usage **biassed** and **biassing** respectively are acceptable alternative spellings.

bicentenary and **bicentennial** *see* **bi-**.

biennial *see* **bi-**.

billion traditionally meant 'one million million' in British English, but in modern usage it has increasingly taken on the American English meaning of 'one thousand million'. When the number of million pounds, etc, is specified, the number immediately precedes the word 'million' without the word 'of', as in 'The firm is worth five billion dollars', but if no number is present then 'of' precedes 'dollars, etc', ' as in 'The research project cost the country millions of dollars'. The word **billion** may also be used loosely to mean 'a great but unspecified number', as in 'Billions of people in the world live in poverty'.

birth name

birth name is a suggested alternative for **maiden name**, a woman's surname before she married and took the name of her husband. **Maiden name** is considered by some to be inappropriate since maiden in one of its senses is another name for 'virgin' and it is now not at all usual for women to be virgins when they marry. Another possible name alternative is **family name.**

biweekly *see* **bi-**.

bizarre, meaning 'odd, weird', is frequently misspelt. Note the single *z* and double *r*.

black is the word now usually applied to dark-skinned people of Afro-Caribbean origins and is the term preferred by most black-skinned people themselves. **Coloured** is considered by many to be offensive since it groups all non-Caucasians together. In America, African-American is becoming increasingly common as a substitute for **black**.

blackguard, meaning 'a wicked or dishonourable person, a scoundrel', has an unusual pronunciation. It is pronounced *blagg*-ard.

blind is objected to by those concerned with 'political correctness' on the grounds that it concentrates on the negative aspect of being without sight. They suggest 'optically challenged' although this has not become widely used.

bloc and **block** are liable to be confused. **Bloc** refers to 'a group of people, parties or countries that get together for a particular purpose, often a political one', as in 'Those countries were formerly members of the communist bloc'. **Block** has a wide range of meanings, as in 'a block of wood', 'a block of cheese', 'an office block', 'a road block'.

blond and **blonde** are both used to mean 'a fair-haired person', but they are not interchangeable. **Blond** is used to describe a man or boy, **blonde** is used to describe a woman or girl. They are derived from the French adjective, which changes endings according to the gender of the noun.

boat and **ship** are often used interchangeably, but usually **boat** refers to a smaller vessel than a ship.

bona fide is an expression of Latin origin meaning literally 'of good faith'. It means 'genuine, sincere' or 'authentic', as in 'a bona fide member of the group', 'a bona fide excuse for not going', or 'a bona fide agreement'.

born-again was originally applied to an evangelical Christian who had been converted. Although this use still exists, the meaning has extended to refer to a conversion to a belief or cause, especially when this is extremely enthusiastic and fervent, as in 'a born-again nonsmoker', 'a born-again conservationist'.

bottom line is an expression from accountancy that has become commonly used in the general language. In accountancy it refers to the final line of a set of company accounts, which indicates whether the company has made a profit or a loss, obviously a very important line. In general English, **bottom line** has a range of meanings, from 'the final outcome or result', as in 'The bottom line of their discussion was that they decided to sell the company', through 'the most important point of something', as in 'The bottom line was whether they could

bouquet

get there on time or not', to 'the last straw', as in 'His affair with another woman was the bottom line of their stormy relationship and she left him'.

bouquet is frequently misspelt and mispronounced. Note the *ou* and *qu* in the spelling. It is pronounced boo-*kay*.

bourgeois, a word meaning middle-class that is usually derogatory, is frequently misspelt. Note the *our* in the first syllable and the *e* before the *ois*.

boycott, meaning 'to refuse to having anything to do with', is frequently misspelt. Note the double *t* at the end of the word.

brackets may be used to enclose any material of a supplementary or explanatory nature that interrupts the flow of a sentence. The material inside the brackets may be removed without altering the central meaning of the sentence. Commas or dashes may be used to serve the same purpose, when the interruption to the flow of the sentence is not quite so marked. Round brackets are more commonly used than square brackets. Examples of brackets include 'Pablo Picasso (1881-1973) was a famous artist'; 'There are a great many people with her family name (Brown) listed in the telephone directory'; 'He has a yucca (a kind of plant) in his study'. **Brackets** are also known as **parentheses** (singular **parenthesis**).

breach and **breech** are liable to be confused. **Breach** means 'a break or gap', as in 'cows getting through a breach in the fence', and 'the breaking or violation of', as in 'commit a breach of the peace', 'a breach of the local bye-laws'. **Breech**, on the other hand, means 'the rear part of the body' as in 'It was a breech delivery (i.e.

the baby was delivered bottom first)', or 'the part of a gun behind the barrel', as in 'a breech-loading gun'.

broach and **brooch** are liable to be confused. They are pronounced alike but have different meanings. **Broach** is a verb meaning either to 'introduce or mention (a subject)', as in 'She did not like to broach the subject of money at the interview', or 'to open (a bottle)', as in 'broach a bottle of champagne to celebrate the baby's birth'. **Brooch** is a noun that means 'a piece of jewellery that one pins on a blouse, sweater, etc.'

brochure is usually pronounced *bro*-sher, despite the *ch* spelling, rather than bro-*shoor*, which is French-sounding. The word is French in origin.

brooch *see* **broach**.

buffet has two different pronunciations according to sense. In the sense of 'a counter or sideboard from which food is served' and 'self-service food set out on tables', as in 'They are having a buffet rather than a sit-down meal at the wedding', **buffet** is pronounced *boo*-fay. **Buffet** also has the meaning of 'to strike', as in 'ships buffeted by the wind', and 'a blow', as in 'give the boy a buffet across the ear', when it is pronounced buf-fet.

buoyant, meaning either 'able to float', as in 'Rubber is a buoyant substance', or 'cheerful', as in 'in buoyant mood', is frequently misspelt. The most common error is to put the *u* and *o* in the wrong order.

bureaucracy is frequently misspelt. Note the *eau* combination and the *c*, not *s*, before *y*.

burned and **burnt** may be used interchangeably as the past tense and the past participle of the verb 'to burn', as

business

in 'They burned/burnt the rubbish in the back garden'
and 'She has burned/burnt her arm on the stove'.

business is frequently misspelt. The most common error
is to omit letter *i* since it is not pronounced.

bus was originally an abbreviation for omnibus but it is
no longer spelt with an apostrophe before it. Thus **bus**,
not **'bus.** The plural is **buses.**

bylaw and **bye-law** are both acceptable spellings. The
word means a law or rule applying to a local area.

C

caffeine, a stimulant found in coffee and tea, is frequently misspelt. Note the double *f* and the *ei* combination. Note also the pronunciation (*kaf*-feen).

calendar, calender and **colander**: **calendar** is often misspelt as **calender**, which is the name of 'a machine used to smooth paper or cloth', or as **calander**, simply an erroneous spelling. **Calendar** is also sometimes confused with **colander**, a perforated bowl used for straining.

can and **may** both mean in one of their senses 'to be permitted'. In this sense **can** is much less formal than **may** and is best restricted to informal contexts, as in '"Can I go to the park now?" asked the child'. **May** is used in more formal contexts, as in 'May I please have your name?' Both **can** and **may** have other meanings. **Can** has the meaning 'to be able', as in 'They thought his legs were permanently damaged but he can still walk'. **May** has the additional meaning 'to be likely', as in 'You may well be right'.

   The past tense of **can** is **could**, as in 'The children asked if they could (= be permitted to) go to the park'. 'The old man could (= be unable to) not walk upstairs'. The past tense of **may** is **might**, as in 'The child asked if he might have a piece of cake (= be permitted to)'. 'They might (= be likely to) well get here tonight'.

cannon

cannon and **canon** are liable to be confused although they
mean completely different things. **Cannon** means 'a large
gun', as in 'large cannons placed on the castle ramparts',
or 'a kind of shot in billiards', as in 'His opponent won
the match with a superb cannon'. **Canon** refers to 'a rul-
ing, particularly one laid down by the church', as in 'accused of breaking the canons of his church' and 'refuse
to obey the traditional moral canons', or to 'a title given
to some clergymen' as in 'one of the cathedral canons'.

cannot, can not, and **can't** all mean the same thing but
they are used in different contexts. **Cannot** is the most
usual form, as in 'The children have been told that they
cannot go' and 'We cannot get there by public trans-
port'. **Cannot** is written as two words only for emphasis, as in 'No, you can not have any more' and 'The
invalid certainly can not walk to the ambulance'. **Can't**
is used in less formal contexts and often in speech, as in
'I can't be bothered going out' and 'They can't bear to
be apart'.

canvas and **canvass** are liable to be confused. **Canvas** is
'a type of heavy cloth', as in 'tents made of canvas',
'trousers made of canvas', and 'paint on canvas'. **Canvass** is a verb meaning 'to solicit votes, orders, etc, from',
as in 'members of various political parties canvassing
people in the high street' and 'encyclopedia salesmen
canvassing our neighbours', and also meaning 'to find
out how people are going to vote in an election, etc', as
in 'Party workers canvassed our street the night before
the election'. **Canvass** may also be a noun, as in 'an
eve-of-election canvass'.

capital letters are used in a number of different situations. The first word of a sentence or a direct quotation begins with a **capital letter**, as in 'They left early', 'Why have they gone?' and 'He said weakly, "I don't feel very well"'.

The first letter of a name or proper noun is always a **capital letter**, as in 'Mary Brown', 'John Smith', 'South America', 'Rome', 'speak Italian', 'Buddhism', 'Marxism'. **Capital letters** are also used in the titles of people, places or works of art, as in 'Uncle Fred', 'Professor Jones', 'Ely Cathedral', Edinburgh University', 'reading *Wuthering Heights*', 'watching *Guys and Dolls*', 'listen to Beethoven's Third Symphony' and 'a copy of *The Potato Eaters* by van Gogh'. They are also used in the titles of wars and historical, cultural and geological periods, as in 'the Wars of the Roses', 'the Renaissance', 'the Ice Age'.

Note that only the major words of titles, etc, are in **capital letters**, words, such as 'the', 'on', 'of', etc, being in lower-case letters.

A **capital letter** is used as the first letter of days of the week, months of the year, and religious festivals, as in 'Monday', 'October', 'Easter', 'Yom Kippur'. It is a matter of choice whether the seasons of the year are given capital letters or not, as in 'spring/Spring', 'autumn/Autumn'.

Apart from 'I', pronouns are lower-case except when they refer to God or Christ, when some people capitalize them, as in 'God asks us to trust in Him'.

Trade names should be spelt with an initial **capital let-**

carburettor

ter, as in 'Filofax', 'Jacuzzi', 'Xerox', 'Biro', 'Hoover'. When verbs are formed from these, they are spelt with an initial lower-case letter, as 'xerox the letter', 'hoover the carpet'.

carburettor is frequently misspelt. Note the single *r* and double *t*.

carcass and **carcase** are both acceptable spellings for the word for the body of a dead animal. The dead body of a human is called a **corpse**.

cardinal and **ordinal** numbers refer to different aspects of numbers. **Cardinal** is applied to those numbers that refer to quantity or value without referring to their place in the set, as in 'one', 'two', 'fifty' 'one hundred'. **Ordinal** is applied to numbers that refer to their order in a series, as in 'first', 'second', 'fortieth', 'hundredth'.

cardigan, jersey, jumper and **sweater** all refer to knitted garments for the top part of the body. **Cardigan** refers to a jacket-like garment with buttons down the front. **Jersey, jumper** and **sweater** refer to a knitted garment pulled over the head to get it on and off.

carer has recently taken on the meaning of 'a person who looks after a sick, handicapped or old relative or friend', as in 'carers requiring a break from their responsibilities'.

caring has recently been used to apply to professions such as social workers, nurses and doctors, and others who are professionally involved in the welfare of people, as in 'the members of the caring professions'.

carpet and **rug** both refer to forms of floor covering. Generally a rug is smaller than a carpet, and the fitted variety of fabric floor covering is always known as carpet.

caster and **castor** are mainly interchangeable. Both forms can be applied to 'a swivelling wheel attached to the base of a piece of furniture to enable it to be moved easily' and 'a container with a perforated top from which sugar is sprinkled'. The kind of sugar known as **caster** can also be called **castor**, although this is less usual. The lubricating or medicinal oil known as **castor oil** is never spelt **caster**.

catarrh is frequently misspelt. Note the single *t*, double *r*, and *h*.

Catholic and **catholic** have different meanings. **Catholic** as an adjective refers to the Roman Catholic Church, as in 'The Pope is head of the Catholic Church', or to the universal body of Christians. As a noun it means 'a member of the Catholic Church', as in 'She is a Catholic but he is a Protestant'. Catholic with a lower-case initial letter means 'general, wide-ranging', as in 'a catholic selection of essays', and ' broad-minded, liberal', as in 'a catholic attitude to the tastes of others'.

ceiling is frequently misspelt. Note the *e* before *i*. As well as its literal use, **ceiling** is used to mean 'upper limit', as in 'impose a ceiling on rent increases'.

celibate means 'unmarried' or 'remaining unmarried and chaste, especially for religious reasons', as in 'Roman Catholic priests have to be celibate'. In modern usage, because of its connection with chastity, **celibate** has come to mean 'abstaining from sexual intercourse', as in 'The threat of Aids has made many people celibate'. The word is frequently misspelt. Note the *i* after *l*.

Celsius

Celsius, **centigrade** and **Fahrenheit** are all scales of temperature. **Celsius** and **centigrade** mean the same and refer to a scale on which water freezes at O° and boils at 100°. This scale is now the principal unit of temperature. **Celsius** is now the more acceptable term. **Fahrenheit** refers to a scale on which water freezes at 32° and boils at 212°. It is still used, informally at least, of the weather, and statements such as 'The temperature reached the nineties today' are still common.

Note the initial capital letters in **Celsius** and **Fahrenheit**. This is because they are named after people, namely the scientists who devised them.

Celtic is usually pronounced kel-tik. It refers to the 'language, people or culture of Scotland, Ireland, Wales and Brittany', as in 'try to preserve the Celtic tradition'.

censor, censure and **censer** are liable to be confused. **Censor** means 'to examine letters, publications, etc, and remove anything whose inclusion is against official policy, or is obscene or libellous', as in 'In wartime, soldiers' letters were often censored in case the enemy got hold of useful information' and in 'Parts of the film had to be censored in order to make it suitable for children'. **Censure** means 'to blame or criticize severely', as in 'The police were censured by the press for not catching the murderer of the child' and in 'The pupils were censured by the headmaster for bullying younger children'. **Censure** may also be a noun, as in 'They encountered strong censure from their neighbours for reprimanding the children'. The spelling of **censor** is often confused with that of **censer**, 'a vessel used for burning incense'.

centenary and **centennial** are both used to refer to a 'one-hundredth anniversary'. **Centenary** is the more common term in British English, as in 'celebrate the town's centenary', whereas **centennial** is more common in American English. **Centennial** may be used as an adjective, as in 'organize the town's centennial celebrations'.

centigrade *see* **Celsius**.

centre and **middle** mean much the same, but **centre** is used more precisely than **middle** in some cases, as in 'a line through the centre of the circle' and 'She felt faint in the middle of the crowd'.

centre on and **centre around** are often used interchangeably, as in 'Her world centres on/around her children'. **Centre around** is objected to by some people on the grounds that **centre** is too specific to be used with something as vague as **around**. When it is used as a verb with place names, **centre** is used with 'at', as in 'Their business operation is centred at London'.

centuries are calculated from 1001, 1501, 1901, etc, not 1000, 1500, 1900, etc. This is because the years are counted from AD 1, there being no year 0.

cervical has two possible pronunciations. Both *ser*-vik-al, with the emphasis on the first syllable, and ser-*vik*-al, with the emphasis on the second syllable which has the same sound as in Viking. The word means 'referring to the neck or the constricted part of an organ, e.g. of the uterus', as in 'cervical cancer'.

chair is often used to mean 'a person in charge of a meeting, committee, etc', as in 'The committee has a new chair this year'. Formerly **chairman** was always used in this context, as in 'He was appointed chairman of the fund-raising committee' but this is disapproved of on the grounds that it is sexist. Formerly, **chairman** was sometimes used even if the person in charge of the meeting or committee was a woman, and sometimes **chairwoman** was used in this situation. **Chairperson**, which also avoids sexism, is frequently used instead of **chair**. **Chair** is also a verb meaning 'to be in charge of a meeting, committee, etc'.

-challenged is a modern suffix that is very much part of politically correct language. It is used to convey a disadvantage, problem or disorder in a more positive light. For example, 'visually challenged' is used in politically correct language instead of 'blind' or 'partially sighted', and 'aurally challenged' is used instead of 'deaf' or 'hard of hearing'. **-Challenged** is often used in humorous coinages, as in 'financially challenged', meaning 'penniless', and 'intellectually challenged', meaning 'stupid'.

chamois is frequently both misspelt and mispronounced. In the sense of 'a kind of cloth (made from the skin of the chamois antelope) used for polishing or cleaning' it is pronounced *sham*-mi. In the sense of 'a kind of antelope', it is pronounced *sham*-wa.

changeable is frequently spelt wrongly. Note the *e* after the *g*.

chaperon and **chaperone** are both acceptable spellings. The word means 'an older woman who accompanies or supervises a young unmarried woman on social occasions', as in 'in Victorian times young unmarried wom-

en did not go out with young men without a chaperon/
chaperone'. The word may also be a verb, as in 'She
was asked to chaperon/chaperone her niece to the ball'.

charisma was formerly a theological word used to mean
'a spiritual gift', such as the gift of healing, etc. In modern usage it is used to describe 'a special quality or power that influences, inspires or stimulates other people,
personal magnetism', as in 'The president was elected
because of his charisma'. The adjective from **charisma**
is **charismatic**, as in 'his charismatic style of leader-
ship'.

charted and **chartered** are liable to be confused. **Charted** is formed from the verb 'to chart', meaning 'to make
a chart or map of', as in 'few charted areas of the conti-
nent'. It is more common in the negative, as in 'unchart-
ed areas of the interior of the country'. **Chartered** has
two meanings. One is formed from the verb 'to charter',
meaning 'to hire', as in 'a chartered yacht'. The other is
usually found in such phrases as 'chartered accountant/
surveyor/engineer, etc', and means 'an accountant, etc,
who has passed the examinations of the Institute of Chartered Accountants, etc'. The institutes in question have
received a royal charter or 'document granting certain
official rights or privileges'.

chauvinism originally meant 'excessive patriotism', being derived from the name of Nicolas Chauvin, a soldier
in the army of Napoleon Bonaparte, who was noted for
his excessive patriotism. In modern usage **chauvinism**
has come to mean 'excessive enthusiasm or devotion to
a cause' or, more particularly, 'an irrational and preju-

check

diced belief in the superiority of one's own cause'. When preceded by 'male', it refers specifically to attitudes and actions that assume the superiority of the male sex and thus the inferiority of women, as in 'accused of not giving her the job because of male chauvinism'. **Chauvinism** is frequently used to mean **male chauvinism**, as in 'He shows his chauvinism towards his female staff by never giving any of them senior jobs'. The adjective formed from **chauvinism** is **chauvinistic**.

check and **cheque** are liable to be confused. **Check** as a verb means 'to make sure that something is in order', as in 'check the tread of the tyres', or 'to make sure', as in 'check you locked the windows', or 'to slow down, stop or control', as 'check the growth of drug-related offences'. As a noun **check** means 'an examination to make sure that something is in order, as in 'conduct checks on all tyre treads', or 'a slowing-down or stopping', as in 'ordering a check on public expenditure', or 'a curb, restraint or check', as in 'His common sense acted as a check on their extravagance'. **Cheque** means 'a money order', as in 'pay his bill by cheque'. In American English **check** is used for 'money order' as well as the other meanings.

chemist and **pharmacist** have the same meaning in one sense of **chemist** only. **Chemist** and **pharmacist** are both words for 'one who prepares drugs ordered by medical prescription'. **Chemist** has the additional meaning of 'a scientist who works in the field of chemistry', as in 'He works as an industrial chemist'.

cheque *see* **check**.

chilblain is frequently misspelt. Note the single *l*.

childish and **childlike** both refer to someone being like a child but they are used in completely different contexts. **Childish** is used in a derogatory way about someone to indicate that he or she is acting like a child in an immature way, as in 'Even though she is 20 years old she has childish tantrums when she does not get her own way' and 'childish handwriting for an adult'. **Childlike** is a term of approval or a complimentary term used to describe something that has some of the attractive qualities of childhood, as in 'She has a childlike enthusiasm for picnics' and 'He has a childlike trust in others'.

chiropodist, meaning 'a person who treats minor disorders of the feet, is usually pronounced kir-*op*-od-ist with an initial *k* sound, but the pronunciation shir-*op*-od-ist with an initial *sh* sound is also possible.

chord and **cord** are liable to be confused because they sound alike. The spelling **chord** is used in the musical sense, as in 'play the wrong chord', and in the mathematical sense, as in 'draw a chord joining the points on the circumference of a circle'. The spelling **cord** is used to mean 'a kind of string', as in 'tie up the bundle with cord' and 'use a piece of nylon cord as a washing line'. Cord is also used with reference to certain parts of the body, as in 'spinal cord', 'vocal cords', umbilical cord'.

Christian name is used to mean someone's first name as opposed to someone's **surname**. It is increasingly being replaced by **first name** or **forename** since Britain has become a multicultural society where there are several religions as well as Christianity.

chronic *see* **acute**.

cirrhosis is liable to be misspelt. Note the *rrh* combination. The word refers to 'a disease of the liver'.

city and **town** in modern usage are usually distinguished on grounds of size and status, a city being larger and more important than a town. Originally in Britain a **city** was a town which had special rights conferred on it by royal charter and which usually had a cathedral.

clandestine, meaning 'secret or furtive', usually has the emphasis on the second syllable, as klan-*des*-tin', but it is acceptable to pronounce it with the emphasis on the first syllable, as *klan*-des-tin.

classism means 'discrimination on the grounds of class, snobbism', as in 'Not letting her children play with the children of her housekeeper was classism'. **Classist** refers to 'a person who practises classism, a snob', as in 'She's such a classist that she is always rude to shop assistants'.

claustrophobia, fear of confined spaces, is frequently misspelt. Note the *au* and the *o* before *p*.

clean and **cleanse** as verbs both mean 'to clean', as in 'clean the house' and 'cleanse the wound'. However, **cleanse** tends to indicate a more thorough cleaning than **clean** and sometimes carries the suggestion of 'to purify', as in 'prayer cleansing the soul'.

cliché is 'a phrase that has been used so often that it has become stale'. Some examples include 'unused to public speaking as I am', 'time heals everything', 'a blessing in disguise', 'keep a low profile', 'conspicuous by their absence', 'part and parcel', 'at death's door'. Sometimes the phrase in question was quite apt when first used but overuse has made it trite and frequently almost meaningless.

client and **customer**, although closely related in meaning, are not interchangeable. **Client** refers to 'a person who pays for the advice or services of a professional person', as in 'They are both clients of the same lawyer', 'a client waiting to see the bank manager' and 'hairdressers who keep their clients waiting'. **Customer** refers to 'a person who purchases goods from a shop, etc', as in 'customers complaining to shopkeepers about faulty goods' and 'a regular customer at the local supermarket'. **Client** is used in the sense of 'customer' by shops who regard it as a more superior word, as in ' clients of an exclusive dress boutique'.

clientele, meaning a group of clients, is frequently both mispronounced and misspelt. It is pronounced klee-on-*tel*. Note the *le*, not double *ll*.

climate no longer refers just to weather, as in 'go to live in a hot climate', 'Britain has a temperate climate'. It has extended its meaning to refer to 'atmosphere', as in 'live in a climate of despair' and to 'the present situation', as in 'businessmen nervous about the financial climate'.

clone originally was a technical word meaning 'one of a group of offspring that are asexually produced and which are genetically identical to the parent and to other members of the group'. In modern usage **clone** is frequently used loosely to mean 'something that is very similar to something else', as in 'In the sixties there were many

Beatles' clones', and 'grey-suited businessmen looking like clones of each other'.

collaborate and **cooperate** are not interchangeable in all contexts. They both mean 'to work together for a common purpose', as in 'The two scientists are collaborating/cooperating on cancer research' and 'The rival building firms are collaborating/cooperating on the new shopping complex'. When the work concerned is of an artistic or creative nature **collaborate** is the more commonly used word, as in 'The two directors are collaborating on the film' and 'The composers collaborated on the theme music'. **Collaborate** also has the meaning of 'to work with an enemy, especially an enemy that is occupying one's country', as in 'a Frenchman who collaborated with the Germans when they installed a German government in France'.

coloured *see* **black**.

coloration, meaning 'arrangement or mode of colouring', as in 'the unusual coloration of the bird', is frequently misspelt. Unlike **colour**, it has no *u* before the *r*.

columnist, meaning 'a person who writes a column, or regular feature, in a newspaper or magazine', as in 'a columnist with the *New York Times*', is liable to be mispronounced. The *n* is pronounced, unlike in **column** where the *n* is silent.

commemorate means 'to remember, or mark the memory of, especially with some kind of ceremony', as in 'commemorate the soldiers who died in the war with an annual church service'. When applied to a plaque, piece of sculpture, etc, it means 'to serve as a memorial to', as in 'The statue in the village square commemorates those who gave their lives in World War II.

commence, begin, and **start** mean the same, but **commence** is used in a more formal context than the other two words, as in 'The legal proceedings will commence tomorrow' and 'The memorial service will commence with a hymn'. **Begin** and **start** are used less formally, as 'The match begins at 2 p.m.' and 'The film has already started'.

commensurate is followed by 'with' to form a phrase meaning 'proportionate to, appropriate to', as in 'a salary commensurate with her qualifications' and 'a price commensurate with the quality of the goods'.

commitment, meaning 'dedication or loyalty', as in 'his commitment to the socialist cause' and 'unable to make the commitment that marriage demands', is frequently misspelt. Note the double *m* but single *t*. Note that **committed** has double *t*.

committee is frequently misspelt. Note the double *m*, double *t* and double *e*. It may be either a singular or plural noun, and so takes either a singular or plural verb, as in 'The committee meets tomorrow' and 'The committee have reached a decision'.

comparable is liable to be mispronounced. The emphasis should be on the first syllable, as in *kom*-par-able. It is often mispronounced with the emphasis on the second syllable.

comparatively means 'relatively, in comparison with a standard', as in 'The house was comparatively inexpensive for that area of the city' and 'In an area of extreme poverty they are comparatively well off'. In modern usage it is often used loosely to mean 'rather' or 'fairly' without any suggestion of reference to a standard, as in 'She has comparatively few friends' and 'It is a comparatively quiet resort'.

compare may take either the preposition 'to' or 'with'. 'To' is used when two things or people are being likened to each other or being declared similar, as in 'He compared her hair to silk' and 'He compared his wife to Helen of Troy'. 'With' is used when two things or people are being considered from the point of view of both similarities and differences, as in 'If you compare the new pupil's work with that of the present class you will find it brilliant', and 'If you compare the prices in the two stores you will find that the local one is the cheaper'. In modern usage the distinction is becoming blurred because the difference is rather subtle.

comparison is usually followed by the preposition 'with', as in 'In comparison with hers his work is brilliant'. However, when it means 'the action of likening something or someone to something or someone else', it is followed by 'to', as in 'the comparison of her beauty to that of Garbo'.

complacent and **complaisant** are liable to be confused because they are pronounced similarly, as kom-*play*-sint and kom-*play*-zint. However, they have slightly different meanings. **Complacent** means 'smug, self-satisfied', as in 'He knows that he has passed the exam and he is very complacent' and 'She gave a complacent smile when she realized that she had won'. **Complaisant** is rather a formal word meaning 'willing to go along with the wishes of others, acquiescent', as in ''She will not raise any objections—she is so complaisant'. 'She indicated her agreement with a complaisant gesture'.

complement and **compliment** are liable to be confused since they sound alike. However, they have totally different meanings. **Complement** refers to 'something that makes something complete', as in 'The wine was the perfect complement to the meal' and 'Her hat and shoes were the ideal complement to her outfit'. It also refers to 'the complete number or quantity required or allowed', as in 'We have our full complement of staff' and 'a full complement of passengers'. When trying to distinguish between **complement** and **compliment** it is helpful to remember the connection between complement and complete since both have *ple* in the middle. **Compliment** is 'an expression of praise, admiration, approval, etc', as in 'pay her a compliment on her hair' and 'receive compliments on the high standard of their work'. **Complement** and **compliment** are also verbs, as in 'The wine complemented the meal very well' and 'He complimented her on her musical performance'.

complementary medicine is a term applied to the treatment of illness or disorders by techniques other than conventional medicine. These include homoeopathy, osteopathy, acupuncture, acupressure, iridology, etc. The word **complementary** suggests that the said techniques complement and work alongside conventional medical techniques. **Alternative medicine** means the same as **complementary medicine**, but the term suggests that

complex

they are used instead of the techniques of conventional medicine rather than alongside them.

complex in one of its senses is used rather loosely in modern usage. It refers technically to 'an abnormal state caused by unconscious repressed desires or past experiences', as in 'an inferiority complex'. In modern usage it is used loosely to describe 'any obsessive concern or fear', as in 'She has a complex about her weight', 'He has a complex about his poor background'. **Complex** is also used to refer to 'a group of connected or similar things'. It is now used mainly of a group of buildings or units connected in some way, as in 'a shopping complex' or 'a sports complex'.

Complex is also an adjective meaning 'complicated', as in 'His motives in carrying out the crime were complex' and 'The argument was too complex for most people to understand'.

compose, comprise and **constitute** are all similar in meaning but are used differently. **Compose** means 'to come together to make a whole, to make up'. It is most commonly found in the passive, as in 'The team was composed of young players' and 'The group was composed largely of elderly people'. It can be used in the active voice, as in 'the tribes which composed the nation' and 'the members which composed the committee', but this use is rarer. **Constitute** means the same as **compose** but it is usually used in the active voice, as in 'the foodstuffs that constitute a healthy diet' and 'the factors that constitute a healthy environment'. **Comprise** means 'to consist of, to be made up of', as in 'The firm comprises six

58

departments' and 'The team comprises eleven players and two reserve players'. It is frequently used wrongly instead of **compose**, as in 'The team is comprised of eleven players' and instead of **constitute**, as in 'the players that comprise a team'.

compulsory and **compulsive** are liable to be confused. They are both adjectives derived from the verb 'to compel', meaning 'to force', but they are used differently. **Compulsory** means 'obligatory, required by a rule, law, etc', as in 'Foreign languages are not compulsory in that school' and 'It is compulsory to wear school uniform in some schools'. **Compulsive** means 'caused by an obsession or internal urge', as in 'a compulsive gambler' and 'a compulsive eater'. It is also used to mean 'fascinating' in some situations, as in 'A compulsive novel' and 'a compulsive TV series'.

concave and **convex** are liable to be confused. **Concave** means 'curved inwards', as in 'The inside of a spoon would be described as concave'. **Convex** means 'curved outwards, bulging', as in 'The outside or bottom of a spoon would be described as convex'.

conducive, meaning 'leading to, contributing to', is followed by the preposition 'to', as in 'conditions conducive to health growth'.

confidant and **confident** are liable to be confused. They sound alike but have different meanings. **Confidant** is rather a rare formal noun referring to 'a person in whom one confides', as in 'The king used two of his most trusted nobles as confidants'. It is derived from French and adds an *e* at the end if the person being confided in is female,

conform

as in 'ladies-in-waiting who were the queen's confi-
dantes'. It has two possible pronunciations. The older
pronunciation has the emphasis on the last syllable (kon-
fi-*dant*). The more modern pronunciation has the emphasis on the first syllable (*kon*-fi-dant). **Confident** is a
common adjective meaning 'self-assured, having confidence', as in 'She looks confident but she is rather an
uncertain person', 'give a confident smile', and 'be confident that he will get the job'.

conform may be followed by the preposition 'to' or the
preposition 'with'. It is followed by 'to' when it means
'to keep to or comply with', as in 'conform to the con-
ventions' and 'refuse to conform to the company regulations', and with 'with' when it means 'to agree with,
to go along with', as in 'His ideas do not conform with
those of the rest of the committee'.

conjurer and **conjuror**, meaning a person who does con-
juring tricks, are both acceptable spellings.

connection and **connexion** are different forms of the same
word, meaning 'a relationship between two things'. In
modern usage **connection** is much the commoner spelling, as in 'no connection between the events' and 'a fire
caused by a faulty connection'.

connoisseur is liable to be misspelt. Note the double *n*
and double *s*, and the *oi*. The word means 'a person having specialized knowledge and judgement on a subject'
as in 'a connoisseur of French wines' and 'a connoisseur of Italian opera'.

conscientious, meaning 'diligent and careful', as in 'conscientious pupils doing their home work', is commonly

misspelt. Note the *t*, which is frequently wrongly omitted.

connote and **denote** are liable to be confused. **Connote** means 'to suggest something in addition to the main, basic meaning of something', as in 'the fear that the word cancer connotes' and 'The word 'home' connotes security and love'. **Denote** means 'to mean or indicate', as in 'The word cancer denotes a malignant illness' and 'The word "home" denotes the place where one lives'.

consequent and **consequential** are liable to be confused. **Consequent** means 'following as a direct result', as in 'He was badly wounded in the war and never recovered from the consequent lameness'. In one of its senses **consequential** has a meaning similar to that of **consequent** in that it means 'following as a indirect result', as in 'She was injured and suffered a consequential loss of earnings'. In this sense **consequential** is usually used in a legal or formal context. **Consequential** also means 'important', as in 'a grave and consequential meeting' and is sometime applied to people when it means 'self-important', as in 'a pompous, consequential little man'.

consequent and **subsequent** are liable to be confused. **Consequent** means 'following as a direct result', as in 'his accident and consequent injuries', while **subsequent** means simply 'happening or occurring after', as in 'their arrival and subsequent speedy departure'.

Consequent is sometimes followed by the preposition 'on' or 'upon', as in 'The court requires him to prove that his disability was consequent upon his accident at work'. **Subsequent** is sometimes followed by the prep-

conservative

osition 'to', as in 'He was a security man subsequent to his retirement from the police'.

conservative when spelt with a lower-case *c* means 'supporting established traditions, institutions, etc, and opposed to great or sudden change', as in 'Some of the members of the amateur dramatics group wanted to stage a modern play this year but the more conservative members opted for a Shakespearian play instead', and 'She would like to go somewhere exotic on holiday but her conservative husband likes to go to the same place every year'. **Conservative** with an initial capital *C* refers to 'a person who is a member or supporter of the Conservative party', as in 'His wife votes Labour but he is a Conservative'. **Conservative** also means 'cautious, moderate', as in 'At a conservative estimate there must have been a thousand people there.

consist can be followed either by the preposition 'of' or by the preposition 'in', depending on the meaning. **Consist of** means 'to be made up of, to comprise', as in 'The team consists of eleven players and two reserve players'. **Consist in** means 'to have as the chief or only element or feature, to lie in', as in 'The charm of the village consists in its isolation' and 'The effectiveness of the plan consisted in its simplicity'.

constitute *see* **compose**.

contagious and **infectious** both refer to diseases that can be passed on to other people but they do not mean the same. **Contagious** means 'passed on by physical contact', as in 'He caught a contagious skin disease while working in the clinic' and 'Venereal diseases are contagious'. **Infectious** means 'caused by airborne or water-borne microorganisms', as in 'The common cold is highly infectious and is spread by people sneezing and coughing'.

contemporary originally meant 'living or happening at the same time', as in 'Shakespeare and Marlowe were contemporary playwrights' and 'Marlowe was contemporary with Shakespeare'. Later it came to mean also 'happening at the present time, current', as in 'What is your impression of the contemporary literary scene?' and 'Contemporary moral values are often compared unfavourably with those of the past'. These two uses of **contemporary** can cause ambiguity. In modern usage it is also used to mean 'modern, up-to-date', as in 'extremely contemporary designs'.

contemptible and **contemptuous** are both adjectives formed from the noun 'contempt', but they are different in meaning. **Contemptible** means 'deserving contempt, despicable', as in 'The contemptible villain robbed the blind man' and 'It was contemptible of her to swindle an old woman'. **Contemptuous** means 'feeling or showing contempt', as in 'their contemptuous attitude to the people they employ' and 'have a contemptuous disregard for the law of the land'.

continual and **continuous** are not interchangeable. **Continual** means 'frequently repeated', as in 'Tired of the continual interruptions he took the telephone off the hook' and 'There were continual complaints from the school about the truancy of their children'. **Continuous** means 'without a break or interruption', as in 'a contin-

contrary

uous period of ill health', 'machines giving off a continuous high-pitched whine' and 'a continuous roll of paper'.

contrary has two possible pronunciations. When it means
'opposite', as in 'hold contrary views', 'traffic going in
contrary directions' and 'On the contrary, I would like
to go very much', it is pronounced with the emphasis on
the first syllable (*kon*-trar-i). When it means 'perverse,
stubborn', as in 'contrary children' it is pronounced with
the emphasis on the second syllable, which is pronounced
to rhyme with 'Mary'.

controversy is usually pronounced with the emphasis on
the first syllable (*kon*-tro-ver-si). In modern usage there
is a growing tendency to place the emphasis on the second syllable (kon-*tro*-ver-si).

convalescence is commonly misspelt. Note the *sc* combination. The word means 'recovery after an illness', as in
'She will have to undergo a long convalescence after
her operation'.

convertible is commonly misspelt. Note the -*ible* spelling.

convex *see* **concave**.

cooperate *see* **collaborate**.

cord *see* **chord**.

co-respondent *see* **correspondent**.

correspondence is frequently misspelt. Note the *ence*. This
is often misspelt as *ance*.

correspondent and **co-respondent** are liable to be confused. **Correspondent** refers either to 'a person who
communicates by letter', as in 'They were correspond-

ents for years but had never met', or to 'a person who
contributes news items to a newspaper or radio or television programme', as in 'the foreign correspondent of
the *Times*'. A **co-respondent** is 'a person who has been
cited in a divorce case as having committed adultery with
one of the partners'.

council and **counsel** sound alike but have different meanings. **Council** refers to 'an assembly of people meeting
for discussion, consultation, administrative purposes,
etc', as in 'the town council' and 'a community council'. **Counsel** means 'advice', as in 'She received wise
counsel from her parents but ignored it'. **Counsel** is also
a verb meaning 'to give advice to', as in he counselled
him on possible careers', 'She was counselled against
leaving school without qualifications'.

councillor and **counsellor** sound alike but have different
meanings. **Councillor** is a member of a council, as in
'town councillors'. **Counsellor** refers to 'a person who
gives advice, especially professional advice on a social
issue', as in 'a debt counsellor' and 'a career counsellor'.

cousin can cause confusion. The children of brothers and
sisters are **first cousins** to each other. The children of
first cousins are **second cousins** to each other. The child
of one's **first cousin** and the **first cousin** of one's parents is one's **first cousin first removed**. The grandchild
of one's **first cousin** or the **first cousin** of one's grand-
parent is one's **second cousin twice removed**.

credible, creditable and **credulous** are liable to be confused. **Credible** means 'believable', as in 'a scarcely

credible story' and 'I do not find her account of the accident credible'. **Creditable** means 'deserving praise', as in 'Despite his injury the athlete gave a very creditable performance'. **Credulous** means 'too ready to believe, gullible', as in 'She was so credulous that she was taken in by the swindler' and 'a credulous young girl believing everything her new boyfriend said'.

crisis literally means 'turning point' and should be used to refer to 'a turning point in an illness', as in 'The fever reached a crisis and she survived' and 'a decisive or crucial moment in a situation, whose outcome will make a definite difference or change for better or worse', as in 'The financial situation has reached a crisis—the firm will either survive or go bankrupt'. In modern usage **crisis** is becoming increasingly used loosely for 'any worrying or troublesome situation', as in 'There's a crisis in the kitchen. The cooker's broken down'. The plural is **crises**.

criterion, meaning 'a standard by which something or someone is judged or evaluated', as 'What criterion is used for deciding which pupils will gain entrance to the school?' and 'The standard of play was the only criterion for entrance to the golf club'. It is a singular noun of which **criteria** is the plural, as in 'They must satisfy all the criteria for entrance to the club or they will be refused'.

critical has two main meanings. It means 'finding fault', as in 'His report on her work was very critical'. It also means 'at a crisis, at a decisive moment, crucial', as in 'It was a critical point in their relationship'. This meaning is often applied to the decisive stage of an illness, as in 'the critical hours after a serious operation', and is used also to describe an ill person who is at a crucial stage of an illness or dangerously ill. **Critical** also means 'involved in making judgements or assessments of artistic or creative works', as in 'give a critical evaluation of the author's latest novel'.

crucial means 'decisive, critical', as in 'His vote is crucial since the rest of the committee is split down the middle'. In modern usage it is used loosely to mean 'very important', as in 'It is crucial that you leave now'. **Crucial** is derived from crux, meaning 'a decisive point', as in 'the crux of the situation'.

cuisine is liable to be misspelt. Note the u before the first i. It is rather a formal word and means 'cooking' or 'a style of cooking', as in 'The cuisine at the new restaurant is outstanding'; 'She prefers Italian cuisine to French cuisine'. Note that it is pronounced kwee-zeen.

curb and **kerb** are not interchangeable although they sound similar. **Curb** is both a noun and a verb. As a noun it means 'control, check, restraint', as in 'act as a curb on his extravagance'. As a verb it means 'to control, to restrain', as in 'She must learn to curb his anger' and 'If he does not learn to curb his expenditure he will become bankrupt'. **Kerb** is a noun meaning 'the edge of a pavement', as in 'The child stood on the kerb waiting to cross the road'. In American English **curb** is used instead of **kerb**.

curriculum is commonly misspelt. Note the double r and single l. The word means 'a programme of educational courses', as in 'The government is making changes to the primary school curriculum' and 'There is a wide range of options on the sixth form curriculum'. **Curriculum** is derived from Latin and originally took the plural form **curricula**, but in modern usage the plural form **curriculums** is becoming common.

curriculum vitae refers to 'a brief account of a person's qualifications and career to date'. It is often requested by an employer when a candidate is applying for a job. **Vitae** is pronounced *vee*-ti, the second syllable rhyming with my.

curtsy and **curtsey** are both acceptable spellings. The word refers to 'a sign of respect in which a woman puts one foot behind the other and bends her knees, sometimes holding her skirt out'.

customer *see* **client**.

D

dais, meaning 'platform' or 'stage', is now usually pronounced as two syllables, as day-is. Formerly it was pronounced as one syllable, as days.

data was formerly used mainly in a scientific or technical context and was always treated as a plural noun, taking a plural verb, as in 'compare the data which were provided by the two research projects'. The singular form was **datum**, which is now rare. In modern usage the word **data** became used in computing as a collective noun meaning 'body of information' and is frequently used with a singular verb, as in 'The data is essential for our research'. This use has spread into the general language.

dates are usually written in figures rather than in words except in formal contexts, such as legal documents. There are various ways of writing dates. The standard form in Britain is becoming day followed by month followed by year, as in '24 February 1970'. In America the standard form of this is 'February 24 1970' and that is a possibility in Britain also. Alternatively, some people write '24th February 1970'. Care should be taken with the writing of dates entirely in numbers, especially if one is corresponding with someone in America. In Britain the day of the month is put first, the month second and the year third, as in '2/3/50', '2 March 1950'. In America the month is put first, followed by the day of the month and the year. Thus in America '2/3/50', would be 3 February 1950.

Centuries may may be written either in figures, as in 'the 19th century' or in words, as in 'the nineteenth century'. Decades and centuries are now usually written without apostrophes, as in '1980s' and '1900s'.

datum *see* **data**.

deadly and **deathly** both refer to death but they have different meanings. **Deadly** means 'likely to cause death, fatal', as in 'His enemy dealt him a deadly blow with his sword' and 'He contracted a deadly disease in the jungle'. **Deathly** means 'referring to death, resembling death', as in 'She was deathly pale with fear'.

decade is pronounced with the emphasis on the first syllable as *dek*-ayd. An alternative but rare pronunciation is dek-*ayd*.

decimate literally means 'to kill one in ten' and is derived from the practice in ancient Rome of killing every tenth soldier as a punishment for mutiny. In modern usage it has come to mean 'to kill or destroy a large part of', as in 'Disease has decimated the population'. It has also come to mean 'to reduce considerably', as in 'the recession has decimated the jobs in the area'.

decry and **descry** are liable to be confused. **Decry** means 'to express criticism or disapproval of, to disparage', as in 'The neighbours decried their treatment of their children' and 'The local people decried the way the police handled the situation'. **Descry** means 'catch sight of', as in 'descry a herd of deer on the horizon'.

defective and **deficient** are similar in meaning but are not interchangeable. **Defective** means 'having a fault, not working properly', as in 'return the defective vacuum cleaner to the shop', 'The second-hand car proved to be defective' and 'He cannot be a pilot as his eyesight is defective'. **Deficient** means 'having a lack, lacking in', as in 'The athlete is very fast but he is deficient in strength' and 'Her diet is deficient in vitamin C.

defence, as in 'soldiers losing their lives in defence of their country' is commonly misspelt. Note the *c*. The word is frequently wrongly spelt with an *s* along the lines of **defensive**. In American English **defence** is spelt **defense**.

deficient *see* **defective**.

definitely is frequently misspelt. Note the *i* before the *t*. It is a common error to put *a* in that position.

delicatessen is liable to be misspelt. Note the single *l*, single *t* and double *s*. It refers to 'a shop selling prepared foods, such as cooked meats, cheeses, etc', as in 'buy some quiche from the local delicatessen'.

deliverance and **delivery** are both nouns formed from the verb 'to deliver' but they are used in different senses. **Deliverance** refers to 'the act of delivering from danger etc, to rescue or save', as in 'thank God for their child's deliverance from the evil kidnappers' and 'pray for their deliverance from evil'. This word is now used only in literary or very formal contexts. **Delivery** has several meanings. It refers to 'the act of delivering letters, goods, etc', as in 'There is no delivery of mail on Sundays' and 'awaiting delivery of a new washing machine'; 'the pro-

delusion

cess of birth', as in 'Her husband was present at the delivery of their son'; 'manner of speaking', as in 'The lecturer's subject was interesting but his delivery was poor'.

delusion and **illusion** in modern usage are often used interchangeably but they are not quite the same. **Delusion** means 'a false or mistaken idea or belief', as in 'He is under the delusion that he is brilliant' and 'suffer from delusions of grandeur'. It can be part of a mental disorder, as in 'He suffers from the delusion that he is Napoleon. **Illusion** means 'a false or misleading impression', as in 'There was no well in the desert—it was an optical illusion', 'The conjurer's tricks were based on illusion' and 'the happy childhood illusions that everyone lived happy ever after'.

demise is a formal word for death, as in 'He never recovered from the demise of his wife'. In modern usage it applies to the ending of an activity, as in 'The last decade saw the demise of coal-mining in the area'. In modern usage it has come to mean also 'the decline or failure of an activity', as in 'the gradual demise of his business'.

demonstrable is most commonly pronounced di-*mon*-strabl, with the emphasis on the second syllable, in modern usage. Previously the emphasis was on the first syllable as *dem*-on-strabl.

dénouement is commonly misspelt. Note the *oue* combination. The first *e* was originally always spelt with an acute accent, as *é*, but in modern usage it is frequently written without the acute. The word means 'the final

72

outcome', as in 'The novel had a unexpected denoue-
ment'. It is pronounced day-*noo*-mon.

dependant and **dependent** are frequently confused. **Dependant** is a noun meaning 'a person who depends on
someone else for financial support', as in 'He has four
dependants—his wife and three children'. **Dependent**
is an adjective meaning 'reliant on', as in 'dependent on
drugs'; 'relying on someone else for financial support',
as in 'have several dependent relatives'; 'decided by,
affected by', as in 'Success in that exam is dependent on
hard work'.

deprecate and **depreciate** are liable to be confused although they have totally different meanings. **Deprecate**
means 'to express disapproval of', as in 'It was unsport-
ing of him to deprecate his rival's performance' and 'deprecate their choice of furnishings'. **Depreciate** means
'to reduce in value', as in 'New cars depreciate very
quickly'. It also means 'to belittle or disparage', as in
'They made great efforts to help but she depreciated
them', 'Management depreciated the role the deputy
manager played in the firm'. In modern usage **deprecate** is sometimes used with the second meaning of **depreciate**, as in 'He was always praising his elder son's
work and deprecating that of his younger son although
the latter was the cleverer pupil'.

deprived means 'having something removed', as in 'The
prisoner was punished by being deprived of his privileges' and 'The fire deprived the children of their home'.
In modern usage it has come to mean 'not having what
are considered to be basic rights, standard of living, etc',

derisive

as in 'deprived children sent to school in worn-out clothes' and 'deprived people living in substandard accommodation'.

derisive and **derisory** are both adjectives connected with the noun 'derision' but they have different meanings. **Derisive** means 'expressing derision, scornful, mocking' as in 'give a derisive smile' and 'His efforts were met with derisive laughter'. Derisory means 'deserving derision, ridiculous' as in 'Their attempts at playing the game were derisory'. **Derisory** is frequently used to mean 'ridiculously small or inadequate', as in 'The salary offered was derisory'.

descry *see* **decry**.

desert and **dessert** are frequent confused. **Desert** as a noun refers to 'a large area of barren land with very little water or vegetation and often sand-covered', as in 'the Sahara Desert'. **Deserts** is a plural noun meaning 'what someone deserves', as in 'The thief who mugged the old lady got his just deserts when he was sent to prison'. As a verb **desert** means 'to abandon', as in 'desert his wife and children' and 'soldiers deserting their post', or 'to fail', as in 'his courage deserted him'. **Dessert** means the last (and sweet) course of a meal, as in 'She served apple pie and cream for dessert'. *See* **dessert**.

desiccated is frequently misspelt. Note the single *s* and double *c*. It means 'dried', as in 'desiccated coconut', or 'lacking animation', as in 'a desiccated old bachelor'.

despatch and **dispatch** are interchangeable. It is most common as a verb meaning 'to send', as in 'despatch/dispatch an invitation'. It is rarer as a noun. It means 'a

74

message or report, often official', as in 'receive a des-patch/dispatch that the soldiers were to move on'. It also means 'rapidity, speed', as in 'carry out the orders with despatch/dispatch'.

desperate is frequently misspelt. Note the *e* before the *r*. It is a common error to put *a* instead.

dessert, pudding, sweet and **afters** all mean the same thing. They refer to the last and sweet course of a meal. **Dessert** has relatively recently become the most wide-spread of these terms. **Pudding** was previously regard-ed by the upper and middle classes as the most accepta-ble word of these, but it is now thought of by many as being rather old-fashioned or as being more suited to certain types of dessert than others—thus syrup sponge would be a pudding, but not fresh fruit salad. **Sweet** is a less formal word and is regarded by some people as be-ing lower-class or regional. **Afters** is common only in very informal English. *See also* **desert**.

detach is often misspelt. Note that there is no *t* before the *ch*.

detract and **distract** are liable to be confused. **Detract** means 'to take away from', as in 'Nothing he could say could detract from her reputation as a writer'. 'The new high-rise buildings detracted from the old-fashioned charm of the village'. **Distract** means 'to take some-one's mind off something, to divert someone's attention', as in 'The golf-player said he lost the match because he was distracted by a dog running on the course'.

device and **devise** are liable to be confused. **Device** is a noun and refers to 'a gadget or tool', as in 'a device for taking stones out of horses' hoofs'. **Devise** is a verb meaning 'to plan, to bring about', as in 'He succeeded in devising a scheme that was certain to succeed'.

devil's advocate is a phrase that is often misunderstood. It means 'someone who points out the possible flaws or faults in an argument etc', as in 'He played the devil's advocate and showed her the weakness in her argument so that she was able to perfect it before presenting it to the committee'. The phrase is sometimes wrongly thought of as meaning 'someone who defends an unpopular point of view or person'.

devise *see* **device**.

diagnosis and **prognosis** are liable to be confused. Both are used with reference to disease but have different meanings. **Diagnosis** refers to 'the identification of a disease or disorder', as in 'She had cancer but the doctor failed to make the correct diagnosis until it was too late'. **Prognosis** refers to 'the prediction of the likely course of a disease or disorder', as in 'According to the doctor's prognosis, the patient will be dead in six months'.

dialect refers to an established form of language confined to an area of a country or to a particular class of people. It includes pronunciation, vocabulary, grammar or sense structure.

dialogue refers to 'a discussion between two or more people'. It usually refers to an exchange of views of people who are involved in a conflict of interest and are trying to reach a compromise, as in 'management and union leaders in dialogue over the factory wages structure' and

'The leaders are engaged in a dialogue to try to prevent a war'.

diarrhoea is frequently misspelt. Note the *rrh* combination and the *oea* combination. The word refers to a very loose bowel movement.

dice was originally the plural form of the singular noun **die**, but **die** is now rarely used. Instead, **dice** is used as both a singular and a plural noun, as in 'throw a wooden dice' and 'use three different dice in the same game'.

dietician and **dietitian** are both acceptable spellings. The word means 'a person who specializes in the principles of nutrition', as in 'hospital dieticians drawing up menus for the patients'.

different is most usually followed by the preposition 'from', as in 'Their style of living is different from ours'. **Different from** is considered to be the most correct construction, particularly in formal English. **Different to** is used in informal situations, as in 'His idea of a good time is different to ours'. **Different than** is used in American English.

differently abled *see* **disabled**.

dilatation and **dilation** are both acceptable forms of the same word formed from the verb 'dilate', meaning 'to expand', as in 'Note the dilatation/dilation of the patient's pupils'.

dilapidated is frequently misspelt. Common errors include putting *t* instead of the middle *d* and substituting *de* at the beginning for *di*.

dilemma is frequently used wrongly. It refers to 'a situation in which one is faced with two or more equally undesirable possibilities', as in 'I can't decide which of the offers to accept. It's a real dilemma'.

dinghy and **dingy** are liable to be confused. **Dinghy** refers to 'a type of small boat', as in 'They went out for a sail in their dinghy'. **Dingy** means 'dirty-looking, gloomy', as in 'colourful curtains to cheer up a dingy room'.

dinner, lunch, supper and **tea** are terms that can cause confusion. Their use can vary according to class, region of the country and personal preference. Generally speaking, people who have their main meal in the evening call it **dinner**. However, people who have their main meal in the middle of the day frequently call this meal **dinner**. People who have **dinner** in the evening usually refer to their midday meal, usually a lighter meal, as **lunch**. A more formal version of this word is **luncheon**, which is now quite a rare word. **Supper** has two meanings, again partly dependent on class and region. It can refer either to the main meal of the day if it is eaten in the evening—when it is virtually a synonym for **dinner**. Alternatively, it can refer to a light snack, such as cocoa and toasted cheese, eaten late in the evening before going to bed. **Tea** again has two meanings when applied to a meal. It either means a light snack-type meal of tea, sandwiches and cakes eaten in the late afternoon. Alternatively, it can refer to a cooked meal, sometimes taken with tea, and also referred to as **high tea**, eaten in the early evening, rather than **dinner** later in the evening.

diphtheria can cause problems both with spelling and pronunciation. Note the *phth* combination in the spelling.

The word, which refers to a type of infectious disease, should be pronounced with an *f* at the end of the first syllable (*dif*) but it is often pronounced with a *p* (*dip*).

disabled is objected to by some people on the grounds that it is a negative term, but it is difficult to find an acceptable alternative. In politically correct language **physically challenged** has been suggested as has **differently abled**, but neither of these has gained widespread use. It should be noted that the use of 'the disabled' should be avoided. 'Disabled people' should be used instead.

disablism and **disableism** mean 'discrimination against disabled people', as in 'He felt his failure to get a job was because of disablism'. **Disablist** and **disableist** are adjectives meaning 'showing or practising disablism', as in 'guilty of disablist attitudes'. They also refer to 'a person who discriminates on the grounds of disability', as in 'That employer is a disablist'.

disadvantaged and **disadvantageous** are both formed from disadvantage but they are used in different senses. **Disadvantaged** means 'not having the standard of living, living conditions or basic rights that others enjoy', as in 'disadvantaged families living in slum conditions'. It means much the same as deprived. **Disadvantageous** means 'causing a disadvantage, unfavourable', as in 'At the end of the first round of the competition the former champion was in a disadvantageous position'.

disappoint is very frequently misspelt. Note the single *s* and double *p*. A common error is to put double *s* and single *p*.

disastrous

disastrous is frequently misspelt. Note that, unlike **disaster** from which it is derived, it has no *e*.

discoloration is frequently misspelt. Note, unlike **colour**, the absence of *u*.

discomfit and **discomfort** are liable to be confused. **Discomfit** is a verb which means 'to disconcert, to embarrass', as in 'They were discomfited by her direct questions', or 'to thwart, to defeat', as in 'He succeeded in discomfiting his opponent'. **Discomfort** is most commonly a noun, although it does exist as a verb. It means 'lack of comfort, lack of ease', as in 'the discomfort of their holiday conditions'.

discover and **invent** are not interchangeable. **Discover** means 'to find something that is already in existence but is generally unknown', as in 'discover a new route to China' and 'discover the perfect place for a holiday'. **Invent** means 'to create something that has never before existed', as in 'invent the telephone' and 'invent a new form of heating system'.

discriminating and **discriminatory** are both formed from **discrimination** but they have different meanings. **Discriminating** means 'able to tell the difference between good and poor quality, etc, having good judgement', as in 'a discriminating collector of antiques' and 'discriminating in their choice of wines'. **Discriminatory** means 'showing or practising discrimination or prejudice', as in 'have a discriminatory attitude towards people of a different race' and 'employers accused of being discriminatory towards women'.

disempowered in modern usage does not mean only 'having one's power removed', as in 'The king was disempowered by the invading general', but also means the same as 'powerless', as in 'We are disempowered to give you any more money'. **Disempowered** is seen in politically correct language as a more positive way of saying **powerless**.

disinterested and **uninterested** are often used interchangeably in modern usage to mean 'not interested, indifferent', as in 'pupils totally *disinterested/uninterested* in school work'. Many people dislike **disinterested** being used in this way and regard it as a wrong use, but it is becoming increasingly common. **Disinterested** also means 'impartial, unbiased', as in 'ask a disinterested party to settle the dispute between them'.

disorient and **disorientate** are used interchangeably. 'The town had changed so much since his last visit that he was completely disoriented/disorientated' and 'After the blow to her head she was slightly disoriented/disorientated'.

disassociate and **dissociate** are used interchangeably, as in 'She wished to disassociate/dissociate herself from the statement issued by her colleagues', but **dissociate** is the more usual.

distinct and **distinctive** are liable to be confused. **Distinct** means 'definite, easily heard, seen, felt, etc', as in 'I got the distinct impression that I had offended him', or 'different, separate', as in 'an artistic style quite distinct from that of his father'. **Distinctive** means 'distinguishing, characteristic', as in 'The zebra has distinctive markings'.

distract

distract *see* **detract**.

divorcee refers to 'a divorced person', as in 'a club for divorcees'. **Divorcé** refers to 'a divorced man', and **divorcée** to 'a divorced woman'.

doubtful and **dubious** can be used interchangeably in the sense of 'giving rise to doubt, uncertain', as in 'The future of the project is dubious/doubtful', and in the sense of 'having doubts, unsure', as in 'I am doubtful/dubious about the wisdom of going'. **Dubious** also means 'possibly dishonest or bad', as in 'of dubious morals'.

downward and **downwards** are not used interchangeably. **Downward** is an adjective, as in 'a downward slope' and 'in a downward direction'. **Downwards** is an adverb, as in 'look downwards from the top of the hill'.

draft and **draught** are liable to be confused. **Draft** as a noun in British English has several meanings. It can mean 'a preliminary version', as in 'present a rough draft of their proposals'; 'a money order', as in 'a draft drawn on a foreign bank'; 'a group of soldiers or other people chosen for a special purpose', as in 'a draft of new recruits sent to the front' and 'a draft of nurses and doctors despatched to the scene of the disaster'. **Draught** as a noun in British English refers to 'a current of air', as in 'a draught from an ill-fitting window', or to 'a drink, a swallow of liquid', as in 'long for a draught of cool beer'. In American English **draught** is spelt **draft**.

drawing room *see* **sitting room**.

draught *see* **draft**.

draughtsman/woman and **draftsman/woman** are not the same. **Draughtsman/woman** refers to 'a person who draws detailed plans of a building, etc', as in 'study the plans of the bridge prepared by the draughtsman'. **Draftsman/woman** refers to 'a person who prepares a preliminary version of plans, etc', as in 'several draftswomen working on the draft parliamentary bills'.

dreamed and **dreamt** are interchangeable both as the past tense and the past participle of the verb 'dream', as in 'She *dreamed/dreamt* about living in the country' and in 'He has dreamed/dreamt the same dream for several nights'.

drier and **dryer** can both be used to describe 'a machine or appliance that dries', as in 'hair-drier/hair-dryer' and 'tumbler drier/dryer'. As an adjective meaning 'more dry', **drier** is the usual word, as in 'a drier summer than last year'.

drunk and **drunken** both mean 'intoxicated' but they are used rather differently. When someone is temporarily intoxicated **drunk** is used, as in 'The drunk men staggered home'. **Drunken** tends to be used to describe someone who is in the habit of being intoxicated, as in 'drunken creatures who are rarely sober'. Otherwise **drunk** is usually used after a verb, as in 'They were all drunk at the party'. **Drunken** is usually used before a noun as in 'take part in a drunken party'.

dryer *see* **drier**.

dubious *see* **doubtful**.

dual and **duel** are liable to be confused since they sound alike. **Dual** is an adjective meaning 'double, twofold', as in 'He played a dual role in the team as captain and trainer' and 'a dual carriageway'. **Duel** is a noun mean-

due to

ing ' a formal fight between two people, using swords
or pistols', as in 'He challenged a fellow officer to a
duel because he had called him a liar'. **Duel** can also be
a verb. The *l* doubles before '-ing', '-ed', or '-er' is added, as in 'duelling at dawn'.

due to, owing to and **because of** should not be used interchangeably. Strictly speaking, **due to** should be used only
adjectivally, as in 'His poor memory is due to brain damage' and 'cancellations due to bad weather'. When a
prepositional use is required **owing to** and **because of**
should be used, as in 'the firm was forced to close owing to a lack of capital' and 'The train was cancelled
because of snow on the line'. In modern usage it is quite
common for **due to** to be used instead of **owing to** or
because of because the distinction is rather difficult to
comprehend.

dyeing and **dying** sound alike but are completely different in meaning. **Dyeing** is formed from the verb 'to dye'
and is used in such contexts as 'dyeing white dresses
blue'. **Dying** is formed from the verb 'to die' and is used
in such contexts as 'dying from starvation'.

E

each, when it is the subject of a sentence, should be followed by a singular verb and, where relevant, by a pronoun in the singular, as in 'Each boy brought his own
lunch'. In order to avoid sexism in language some people advocate using a plural pronoun instead, as in 'Each
pupil had their own books'. Before sexism in language
became an issue, the assumption was that words such as
pupil, which can indicate members of either sex, should
take a male pronoun, as in 'Each pupil had his own
books'. People who dislike using a plural pronoun with
each on the grounds that it is ungrammatical but do not
wish to be sexist can use 'his/her', as in 'Each pupil had
his/her own books' although this device can be clumsy.
It is often possible to avoid the problem by rephrasing
the sentence, as in 'All the pupils had their own books'.
When **each** follows a plural noun or pronoun, the verb
should be plural as in 'The houses each have a red door'
and 'They each have black hair'.

each other and **one another** used not to be used interchangeably. It was taught that **each other** should be used
when only two people are involved and that **one another** should be used when more than two people are involved, as in 'John and Mary really love each other' and

earthly

'All the members of the family love one another'. In modern use this restriction is often ignored.

earthly and **earthy** are both adjectives formed from 'earth' but they have different meanings. **Earthly** is used to refer to this world rather than to heaven or the spiritual world, as in 'He is interested only in earthly pleasures but his brother is interested in spiritual satisfaction'. It is also used informally to mean 'possible', as in 'What earthly reason could she have for leaving?' **Earthy** refers to earth in the sense of 'soil', as in 'the earthy smell of a garden after rain'. It can also mean 'unrefined, coarse', as in 'an earthy sense of humour'.

EC and **EEC** both refer to the same thing, but **EC**, the abbreviation for **Economic Community** has now replaced **EEC**, the abbreviation for **European Economic Community.**

economic and **economical** are both connected with the noun 'economy' but they have different meanings. **Economic** means 'referring to or relating to the economy or economics', as in 'the government's economic policies' and 'studying economic theory'. **Economical** means 'thrifty, avoiding waste', as in 'She is a very economical housekeeper', and 'cheap', as in 'It is more economical for four of us to go by car than by train'. The phrase **economical with the truth** is a less forthright way of saying 'lying', as in 'politicians accused of being economical with the truth'.

ecstasy, meaning 'great joy', is frequently misspelt. Note the *cs* and *as*. Ecstasy, spelt with a capital *E*, is also the name of a non-medicinal drug, associated with raves, professionally organized large-scale parties for young people.

effect *see* **affect**.

effeminate *see* **female**.

e.g. means 'for example' and is an abbreviation of the Latin phrase *exempli gratia*. It is used before examples of something just previously mentioned, as in 'He cannot eat dairy products, e.g. milk, butter and cream'. A comma is usually placed just before it and, unlike some abbreviations, it has full stops.

egoist and **egotist** are frequently used interchangeably in modern usage. Although they are not, strictly speaking, the same, the differences between them are rather subtle. **Egoist** refers to 'a person intent on self-interest, a selfish person', as in 'an egoist who never gave a thought to the needs of others'. **Egotist** refers to 'a person who is totally self-centred and obsessed with his/her own concerns', as in 'a real egotist who was always talking about herself'.

eighth is frequently misspelt. Note the *h* before the *t*.

either should be used only when referring to two people or things, as in 'He hasn't been in touch with either of his parents for several years', but 'He hasn't been in touch with any of his four brothers'.

Either as an adjective or a pronoun takes a singular verb, as in 'Either parent will do' and 'Either of you can come'.

In the **either ... or** construction, a singular verb is used if both parts of the construction are singular, as in 'Either Jane or Mary is in charge'. If both parts are plural

eke out

the verb is plural, as in 'Either their parents or their grandparents are in charge.' If the construction involves a
mixture of singular and plural the verb traditionally
agrees with the subject that is nearer it, as in 'Either her
mother or her grandparents are in charge' and 'Either
her grandparents or her mother is in charge'. If pronouns
are used, the nearer one governs the verb, as in 'Either
they or he is at fault' and 'Either she or they are at fault'.
See **neither**.

eke out originally meant 'to make something more ade-
quate by adding to it or supplementing it', as in 'The
poor mother eked out the small amount of meat with a
lot of vegetables to feed her large family'. It can now
also mean 'to make something last longer by using it
sparingly', as in 'try to eke out our water supply until
we reach a town', and 'to succeed or make with a great
deal of effort', as in 'eke out a meagre living from their
small farm'.

elder and **older** are not interchangeable. **Elder** is used
only of people, as in 'The smaller boy is the elder of the
two'. It is frequently used of family relationships, as in
'His elder brother died before him'. **Older** can be used
of things as well as people, as in 'The church looks ancient but the castle is the older of the buildings' and 'The
smaller girl is the older of the two'. It also can be used
of family relationships, as in 'It was his older brother
who helped him'. **Elder** used as a noun suggests experience or worthiness as well as age, as in 'Important issues used to be decided by the village elders' and 'Children should respect their elders and betters'.

elderly, as well as meaning 'quite or rather old', as in 'a town full of middle-aged and elderly people', is a more polite term than 'old', no matter how old the person referred to is, as in 'a residential home for elderly people'. **Elderly** is used only of people, except when used humorously, as in 'this cheese is getting rather elderly'.

eldest and **oldest** follow the same pattern as **elder** and **older**, as in 'The smallest boy is the eldest of the three', 'His eldest brother lived longer than any of them', 'The castle is the oldest building in the town' and 'He has four brothers but the oldest one is dead'.

elemental and **elementary** are both connected with the noun 'element' but they are not interchangeable. **Elemental** means 'like the elements (in the sense of forces of nature), powerful, uncontrolled', as in 'give way to elemental passion'. It also means 'basic, essential', as in 'the elemental truths of Buddhism'. **Elementary** means 'basic, introductory', as in 'teaching elementary maths', and 'easy, simple', as in 'He cannot carry out the most elementary of tasks' and 'The test is very elementary'.

embarrass is very frequently misspelt. Note the double *r* and double *s*. Note also **embarrassed** and **embarrassing**. The word means 'to cause to feel self-conscious, confused or ashamed', as in 'His extravagant compliments embarrassed her'.

emigrant and **immigrant** are liable to be confused. **Emigrant** refers to 'a person who leaves his/her native land to go and live elsewhere', as in 'go down to the docks to say farewell to the emigrants on the ship'. **Immigrant** refers to 'a person who arrives to live in another country, having left his/her native land', as in 'go down to the docks to welcome the immigrants arriving on the ship'. Both terms can apply to the same person, viewed from different points of view.

emotional and **emotive** are both connected with the noun 'emotion' but they have different meanings. **Emotional** means 'referring to emotion', as in 'emotional problems', 'expressing emotion or excessive emotion', as in 'an emotional farewell', and 'having emotions that are easily excited', as in 'The rest of the family are very calm but she is so emotional that she is always either in tears or laughing with joy'. **Emotive** means 'causing emotion', as in 'Child abuse is often an emotive subject'.

empathy and **sympathy** are liable to be confused although they are not interchangeable. **Empathy** means 'the ability to imagine and share another's feelings, experiences, etc', as in 'As a single parent herself, the journalist has a real empathy with women bringing up children on their own' and 'The writer felt a certain empathy with the subject of his biography since they both came from a poverty-stricken childhood'. **Sympathy** means 'a feeling of compassion, pity or sorrow towards someone', as in 'feel sympathy for homeless children' and 'show sympathy towards the widow'.

encyclopaedia and **encyclopedia** are now both acceptable spellings in modern British English. **Encyclopaedia** is the traditional spelling in British English but the traditional spelling in American English, **encyclopedia**, is now becoming more and more common in British English.

endemic is usually used to describe a disease and means 'occurring in a particular area', as in 'a disease endemic to the coastal areas of the country' and 'difficult to clear the area of endemic disease'.

enervate is a word that is frequently misused. It means 'to weaken, to lessen in vitality', as in 'she was enervated by the extreme heat' and 'Absence of funding had totally enervated the society'. It is often wrongly used as though it meant the opposite.

enormity and **enormousness** are liable to be confused but mean different things. **Enormity** means 'outrageousness or wickedness', as in 'The whole village was shocked by the enormity of his crime'. **Enormousness** means 'the quality of being enormous or extremely large', as in 'The little boy was scared by the enormousness of the elephant' and 'the enormousness of their estates'.

enquiry and **inquiry** are frequently used interchangeably, as in 'make enquiries/inquiries about her health'. However some people see a distinction between them and use **enquiry** for ordinary requests for information, as in 'make enquiries about the times of trains'. They use **inquiry** only for 'investigation', as in 'The police have begun a murder inquiry' and 'launch an inquiry into the hygiene standards of the food firm'.

enrol is frequently misspelt. Note the single *l*, but note also that the *l* doubles in the past tense and past participle and the present participle, as **enrolled, enrolling**. However, the noun **enrolment**, as in 'The enrolment of students takes place tomorrow', has a single *l*. In American English the word is spelt **enroll**. **Enrol** means 'to

enthral

become a member of a class, society, etc, as in 'She plans
to enrol in an aerobics class' and 'to make a member of
a class, society, etc, as in 'The tutor will enrol more students next week'.

enthral is frequently misspelt. Note the single *l*, but note
that the *l* doubles in the past tense and past participle
and the present participle, as **enthralled** and **enthral-
ling**. However, note the single *l* in **enthralment**. In American English the word is spelt **enthrall**. **Enthral** means
'to bewitch, to capture the attention of', as in 'Her performance will enthral the critics'.

envelop and **envelope** are not interchangeable. **Envelop**
means 'to wrap up, to enclose, to surround completely',
as in 'He enveloped his daughter in his arms' and 'Mist
enveloped the mountain tops'. **Envelope** means 'a paper wrapper for a letter, etc', as in 'put the sheets of paper in a large envelope'. **Envelop** is pronounced en-*vel*-
op. The preferred pronunciation of envelope is *en*-vel-
op although some people pronounce it *on*-vel-op.

enviable and **envious** are both formed from the noun
'envy' but they mean different things. **Enviable** means
'arousing envy, desirable', as in 'an enviable lifestyle'
and 'an enviable optimistic attitude to life'. **Envious**
means 'showing or expressing envy', as in 'envious eyes
following the expensively dressed woman' and 'They
were envious of her lifestyle'.

equable and **equitable** are liable to be confused. **Equable** means 'moderate, not given to extremes', as in
'live in an equable climate' and 'have an equable temperament'. **Equitable** means 'fair, just', as in 'We felt

that the judge had come to an equitable decision'.

equal can be followed either by the preposition 'with' or the preposition 'to', but the two constructions are not interchangeable. **Equal to** is used in such sentences as 'He wished to climb the hill but his strength was not equal to the task'. **Equal with** is used in such sentences as 'After many hours of playing the two players remained equal with each other' and 'The women in the factory are seeking a pay scale equal with that of men'.

equally should not be followed by 'as'. Examples of it used correctly include 'Her brother is an expert player but she is equally talented' and 'He is trying hard but his competitors are trying equally hard'. These should not read 'but she is equally as talented' nor 'but his competitors are trying equally as hard'.

Esq. is the abbreviation for 'Esquire'. It is sometimes used rather formally when addressing a letter to a man, as in 'Peter Jones, Esq.' It should not be used with Mr. 'Mr Peter Jones, Esq.' is wrong.

-ess is a suffix that used routinely to be added to a noun to form the femine form, as in 'authoress, editress, poetess, sculptress'. This practice is now often seen as patronizing to women and sexist, and **-ess** is being used less and less. What were once considered masculine forms, as 'author, editor, poet, sculptor', are now considered to be neutral forms applying to either sex. The suffix is still found in such words as 'princess', 'countess', 'hostess' and 'waitress', and sometimes in 'actress'.

et al is the abbreviation of the Latin phrase *et alii*, meaning 'and others'. It is used in lists to indicate that there are more of the same, as in 'She loves Bach, Beethoven, Mozart et al'. The phrase is usually used in a formal context, but it is sometimes used humorously in informal contexts as in 'Uncle Fred, Uncle Jim et al'.

etc is the abbreviation of the Latin phrase *et cetera*, meaning 'and other things, and the rest', as in 'potatoes, carrots, turnips, etc', 'curtains, carpets, rugs, etc'. It can also be spelt **etc.** (with a full stop).

ethnic is a word that causes some confusion. It means 'of a group of people classified according to race, nationality, culture, etc', as in 'a cosmopolitan country with a wide variety of ethnic groups'. It is frequently used loosely to mean 'relating to race', as in 'violent clashes thought to be ethnic in origin', or 'foreign' as in 'prefer ethnic foods to British foods'.

euphemism is 'a more indirect, pleasanter, milder, etc, way of saying something'. 'To join one's forefathers' is a **euphemism** for 'to die'. 'To be tired and emotional' is a euphemism for 'to be drunk'.

evade and **avoid** are similar in meaning but not identical. **Evade** means 'to keep away from by cunning or deceit', as in 'The criminal evaded the police by getting his friend to impersonate him'. **Avoid** means simply 'to keep away from', as in 'Women avoid that area of town at night'.

evasion and **avoidance** are frequently applied to the nonpayment of income tax but they are not interchangeable. Tax **avoidance** refers to 'the legal nonpayment of tax by clever means'. Tax **evasion** refers to 'the illegal means of avoiding tax by cunning and dishonest means'.

even should be placed carefully in a sentence since its

position can influence the meaning. Compare 'He didn't even acknowledge her' and 'He didn't acknowledge even her'. and 'He doesn't even like Jane , let alone love her' and 'He hates the whole family—he doesn't like even Jane'. This shows that **even** should be placed immediately before the word it refers to in order to avoid ambiguity. In spoken English people often place it where it feels most natural, before the verb as in 'He even finds it difficult to relax on holiday'. To be absolutely correct this should be 'He finds it difficult to relax even on holiday' or 'Even on holiday he finds it difficult to relax'.

ever is sometimes added to 'who', 'what', where, etc', as a separate word for emphasis, as in 'Who ever did that terrible thing?' and 'Where ever did you find that?'. Where there is no question of emphasis, **ever** is joined on to the relevant pronoun. Examples include 'Whoever she is, she must be a bad mother' and 'Wherever he goes she goes'.

every is used with singular nouns. Related words, such as verbs and pronouns, are in the singular too, as in 'Every man must provide his own work clothing'. Some people use a plural pronoun in certain situations in order to avoid sexism in language, as in 'Every worker must supply their own work clothing'. This is to avoid the sexism of 'Every worker must supply his own clothing'. It is possible to avoid both sexism and ungrammatical constructions by using 'Every worker must supply his/her clothing', which can be rather clumsy. Alternatively, the whole sentence can be put in the plural, as in 'All the workers must supply their own work clothing'.

everybody and **everyone** can be used interchangeably. They both take singular verbs, as in 'Everyone has expressed the wish to stay' and 'Everybody wishes the war to end'. **Every one** as two words is used when emphasis is required, as in 'Every one of the workers wanted to stay' and 'Every one of the machines was damaged'.

ex- as a prefix means 'former', as in 'the ex-manager' and 'his ex-wife'. It is usually attached to the noun it describes with a hyphen. As a noun, used informally, **ex** means 'former wife, husband or partner'. as in 'He still visits his ex'. **Ex-directory** means 'not listed in the telephone directory', as in 'choose to have an ex-directory number after having received a series of nuisance calls'.

exaggerate is liable to be misspelt. Note the double *g* and single *r*. Note also the *e* before the *r*. The word means 'to describe as being larger, greater, etc, than is the case', as in 'exaggerate the difficulty of the job' and 'exaggerate how poor he is'.

exceedingly and **excessively** are not the same. **Exceedingly** means 'extremely, to a very great extent', as in 'She was exceedingly beautiful' and 'It was exceedingly kind of them to help'. **Excessively** means 'immoderately, to too great an extent, beyond measure', as in 'It was excessively annoying of him to interfere' and 'He was excessively fond of alcohol'.

except is commoner than **except for**. **Except** is used in such sentences as 'They are all dead except his father', 'He goes every day except Sunday'. **Except for** is used at the beginning of sentences, as in 'Except for Fred, all the workers were present', and where **except** applies to a longish phrase, as in 'There was no one present except for the maid cleaning the stairs' and 'The house was silent except for the occasional purring of the cat'. When followed by a pronoun, this should be in the accusative or objective, as in 'There was no one there except *him*' and 'Everyone stayed late except *me*'.

exceptionable and **exceptional** are both related to the noun 'exception' but they mean different things. **Exceptionable** describes something that someone might take exception to or object to, as in 'They found his behaviour exceptionable' and 'behaviour that was not at all exceptionable'. **Exceptional** means 'out of the ordinary, unusual', as in 'an exceptional talent'. It often means 'unusually good, superior', as in 'have an exceptional singing voice' and 'serve exceptional food and drink'.

excessively *see* **exceedingly**.

exercise and **exorcise** are liable to be confused because they sound alike. However, they are completely different in meaning. **Exercise** as a noun means 'physical exertion', as in 'sitting in front of the television taking little exercise' or 'a set of energetic movements' as in 'doing exercises in the morning'. It can also mean 'a piece of school work', as in 'pupils completing maths exercises'.

It is as a verb that **exercise** is most likely to be confused with **exorcise**. **Exercise** as a verb means 'to take part in physical exertion', 'to perform a series of energetic movements', as in 'The girls liked to exercise to music'. It also means 'to make use of, to employ', as in 'He was charged with the offence but exercised his right to remain silent'. **Exorcise** means 'to rid of evil spirits', as in 'ask a priest to exorcise the haunted house'. **Exercise** and **exorcise** are both frequently misspelt. It is a common error to put a *c* after the *x* in both words. Note that **exercise** is not one of the verbs that can end in -*ize*.

exhausting and **exhaustive** are both formed from the verb 'exhaust' but they mean different things. **Exhausting** means 'extremely tiring', as in 'an exhausting climb up the hill' and 'have an exhausting day at the office'. **Exhaustive** means 'thorough, comprehensive', as in 'police making an exhaustive search of the grounds for the murder weapon'.

exhilarate is often misspelt. Note the *lar* combination. It is a common error to put *ler*. The word means 'to make excited, to rouse, to thrill', as in 'exhilarated by a drive in a fast car', 'exhilarated by their walk in the hills'.

expeditious and **expedient** are liable to be confused but have quite different meanings. Expeditious means 'rapid', as in 'send the parcel by the most expeditious method possible'. **Expedient** means 'most convenient, most advantageous', as in 'The government was only interested in what was politically expedient' and 'choose the most expedient method, no matter how immoral'.

explicable is now usually pronounced with the emphasis on the second syllable (ex-*plik*-ibl). Formerly it was commonly pronounced with the emphasis on the first syllable (*ex*-plikibl).

explicit and **implicit** are liable to be confused although they are virtually opposites. **Explicit** means 'direct, clear', as in 'The instructions were not explicit enough' and 'Give explicit reasons for your decision'. **Explicit** is often used in modern usage to mean 'with nothing hidden or implied', as in 'explicit sex scenes'. **Implicit** means 'implied, not directly expressed', as in 'There was an implicit threat in their warning' and 'an implicit criticism in his comments on their actions'. **Implicit** also means 'absolute and unquestioning', as in 'an implicit faith in his ability to succeed' and 'an implicit confidence in her talents'.

exquisite has two possible pronunciations. It is most usually pronounced with the emphasis on the first syllable (*ex*-kwis-it) but some prefer to put the emphasis on the second syllable (iks-*kwis*-it). The word means 'beautiful, delicate', as in 'exquisite jewellery' and 'exquisite workmanship'. It can also mean 'acute', as in 'the exquisite pain of rejected love'.

extant and **extinct** are liable to be confused although they are opposites. **Extant** means 'still in existence', as in 'customs of ancient origin that are still extant in the village', 'a species of animal that is no longer extant'. **Extinct** means 'no longer in existence', as in 'Dinosaurs have been extinct for millions of years', and 'no longer active', as in 'extinct volcanoes' and 'extinct passion'. Note the spelling of **extinct**, which is frequently misspelt.

extinct *see* **extant**.

extinguish is frequently misspelt. Note the *gui* combination. The word means 'to put out, to cause to stop burning', as in 'firemen extinguishing the flames' and 'extinguish the passion'.

extraordinary

extraordinary can cause problems with pronunciation and spelling. The *a* is silent in the pronunciation. Note the *a* before *o* in the spelling. Remember it is made up of 'extra' and 'ordinary'.

extravagant is frequently misspelt. Note the single *g*.

extrovert and **introvert** are liable to be confused although they are opposites. **Extrovert** refers to 'a person who is more interested in what is going on around him/her than in his/her own thoughts and feelings, such a person usually being outgoing and sociable', as in 'She is a real extrovert who loves to entertain the guests at parties'. **Introvert** refers to 'a person who is more concerned with his/her own thoughts and feelings than with what is going around him/her, such a person usually being shy and reserved', as in 'an introvert who hates having to speak in public' and 'introverts who prefer to stay at home than go to parties'. Both **extrovert** and **introvert** can be adjectives as well as nouns, as in 'extrovert behaviour' and 'introvert personality. Note the spelling of **extrovert.** It was formerly spelt with an *a* instead of an *o*.

F

façade can cause problems both with regard to spelling and pronunciation. It is French in origin and, although it has been part of the English language for some time, it still usually retains the cedilla under the *c* (*ç*). In modern usage there is a growing tendency to punctuate less and less, and as this tendency also applies to the use of accents **facade** is also found. The word is pronounced fa-*sahd* and means 'front', as in 'a building with an imposing façade', and 'outward appearance', as in 'hide her grief behind a façade of happiness'.

facetious is commonly misspelt. Note that the vowels appear in alphabetical order (*aeiou*). It means 'humorous, flippant', as in 'You shouldn't make facetious remarks about so grave a subject' and 'a facetious young woman who does not take anything seriously'.

facility and **faculty** are liable to be confused in the sense of 'ability'. **Facility** means 'ease or skill in doing something', as in 'admire his facility with words'. **Faculty** means 'a particular natural talent or power', as in 'her faculty for learning foreign languages'. **Facility** also means 'something that makes it possible or easier to do something'. In this sense it is usually plural (**facilities**), when it often refers to equipment or buildings, as in 'sports facilities'. **Facilities** is sometimes used to mean 'toilet', as in 'Ask the garage owner if we can use his facilities'.

fahrenheit *see* **Celsius.**

family name is used in politically correct language instead of **maiden name** since this is thought to imply that all women are virgins before they are married. Thus 'Her family name was Jones' would be used instead of 'Her maiden name was Jones'. Another politically correct term is **birth name**, as in 'Her birth name was Jones'.

faint and **feint** are sometimes confused. **Faint** as an adjective means either 'not clear, not strong', as in 'hear a faint noise' and 'bear a faint resemblance', or 'giddy, feeling as though one were about to lose consciousness', as in 'She asked if she could sit down as she felt faint'. As a verb it means 'to lose consciousness', as in 'She turned pale and fainted'. As an adjective **feint** is used on stationery to mean 'with faintly printed fine lines', as in 'a pad with feint pages'. In this sense **feint** is sometimes spelt **faint**. **Feint** as a noun means 'a pretended movement intended to distract someone', as in 'His opponent was misled when the boxer made a feint with his left fist'.

fait accompli is a French phrase that has been adopted into English. It refers to 'something that has been done and cannot be undone or changed', as in 'Her parents disapproved of him but by the time they found about the wedding it was a fait accompli and there was nothing they could do about it'. It is pronounced fayt a-kom-*plee*.

fantastic literally means 'relating to fantasy, fanciful, strange', as in 'fantastic dreams' and 'tales of fantastic events'. In modern usage it is often used informally to mean 'exceptionally good, excellent', as in 'have a fantastic holiday' and 'be a fantastic piano player'. It can also mean in informal usage 'very large', as in 'pay a fantastic sum of money'.

farther and **further** are not used interchangeably in all situations in modern usage. **Farther** is mainly restricted to sentences where physical distance is involved, as in 'It is farther to Glasgow from here than it is to Edinburgh'. **Further** can also be used in this sense, as in 'It is further to the sea than I thought'. When referring to time or extent, **further** is used, as in 'Further time is required to complete the task' and 'The police have ordered further investigations'. It can also mean 'additional', as in 'We shall require further supplies'. **Further**, unlike **farther**, can be used as a verb to mean 'to help the progress or development about', as in 'further the cause of freedom'.

fascinate is often misspelt. Note the *c* after the *s*. The word means 'to attract greatly, to capture the attention of', as in 'They were fascinated by the explorer's tales of adventure'.

fatal and **fateful** are liable to be confused although they mean different things. **Fatal** means 'causing death', as in 'involved in a fatal accident' and 'contract a fatal illness', or 'causing ruin or disaster', as in 'His plans for expansion proved fatal to the company' and 'The thief made a fatal mistake and was caught by the police'. **Fate-**

faux pas

ful means 'important and decisive, having important consequences', as in 'He never arrived home on that fateful night' and 'They eventually got married after that first fateful meeting'.

faux pas is a French phrase that has been adopted into the English language. It means 'a social blunder, an indiscreet or embarrassing remark or deed', as in 'The hostess made a faux pas when she asked after her guest's wife, not knowing that they had divorced last year'. **Faux** is pronounced to rhyme with *foe*, and **pas** is pronounced *pa*.

fax is an abbreviation of 'facsimile' and refers to 'an electronic system for transmitting documents using telephone lines'. As a noun **fax** can refer to the machine transmitting the documents, as in 'the fax has broken down again'; to the system used in the transmission, as in 'send the report by fax'; and the document or documents so transmitted, as in 'He replied to my fax at once'.

faze and **phase** are liable to be confused because they sound alike. However, they have totally different meanings. **Faze** is a verb meaning 'to fluster or disconcert', as in 'He was completely fazed by the interviewer's question—he could think of nothing to say'. **Phase** is primarily a noun meaning 'stage', as in 'the next phase of the development plans' and 'teachers going through a defiant phase'. **Phase** can also be a verb, found principally in the phrases **phase in** and **phase out**, which mean respectively 'to introduce gradually' and 'to withdraw gradually', as in 'The changes in the educational system are to be phased in over three years' and 'The old system of staffing will be phased out over the next few months'.

fearful and **fearsome** are both adjectives derived from the noun 'fear' but they mean different things. **Fearful** means 'scared, nervous', as in 'fearful children stumbling through the dark woods' and 'The burglars were fearful of being sent to prison'. It also means informally 'very bad, terrible', as in 'what a fearful mess he's in!' **Fearsome** means 'causing fear, frightening', as in 'fearsome wild animals' and 'It was a fearsome sight to behold'.

feasible is liable to be misspelt. Note the '*-ible*' ending. It means 'capable of being done or achieved, practicable', as in 'trials being carried out to find out if the suggested project is feasible'. In modern usage it is frequently used rather loosely to mean 'possible, probable or likely', as in 'It is just feasible that it might rain'.

February causes problems both with spelling and pronunciation. With reference to spelling note the first *r* between the *b* and *u*. It is a common error to omit this. The correct pronunciation is *feb*-roo-ari, but this is often simplified in informal speech to *feb*-ra-ri.

feint *see* **faint**.

ferment and **foment** can both mean 'to excite, to stir up', as in 'Troublemakers out to ferment discontent' and 'People out to foment trouble in the crowd'. Both words have other meanings that do not relate to each other. **Ferment** means 'to undergo the chemical process known as fermentation', as in 'home-made wine fermenting in the basement'. **Foment** means 'to apply warmth and mois-

fetid

ture to in order to lessen pain or discomfort', as in 'foment the old man's injured hip'.

fetid has two possible pronunciations and two possible spellings. The first syllable can rhyme either with 'met' or 'meet'. With reference to spelling, **foetid** is a rarer alternative spelling.

fête is French in origin and is usually spelt, even in English, with a circumflex over the first *e*. It means 'an outdoor entertainment with the sale of goods, amusement stalls, etc, often held to make money for charity or a good cause', as in 'The proceeds of the village fête went towards the repair of the church roof'. It can be pronounced either to rhyme with 'mate' or 'met'. **Fête** can also be a verb meaning 'to honour or entertain lavishly', as in 'the winning football team were fêted by the whole town when they returned home'.

fetus *see* **foetus**.

female, feminine and **feminist** all relate to women but they are by no means interchangeable. **Female** refers to the sex of a person, animal or plant, as in 'the female members of the group', 'the female wolf and her cubs' and 'the female reproductive cells'. It refers to the child-bearing sex and contrasts with 'male'. **Feminine** means 'having qualities that are considered typical of women or are traditionally associated with women', as in 'wear feminine clothes', 'take part in supposedly feminine pursuits, such as cooking and sewing' and 'feminine hairstyles'. It is the opposite of 'masculine'. It can be used of men as well as women, when it is usually derogatory, as in 'He has a very feminine voice' and 'He walks in a very feminine way'. When applied in a derogatory way to a man, **feminine** means much the same as **effeminate**. **Feminine** also applies to the gender of words, as in 'Lioness is the feminine form of lion'. **Feminist** means 'referring to feminism', 'feminism' being 'a movement based on the belief that women should have the same rights, opportunities, etc', as in 'management trying to avoid appointing anyone with feminist ideas' and 'Equal opportunities is one of the aims of the feminist movement'.

few and **a few** do not convey exactly the same meaning. **Few** is used to mean the opposite of 'many', as in 'We expected a good many people to come but few did' and 'Many people entered the competition but few won a prize'. The phrase **a few** is used to mean the opposite of 'none', as in 'We didn't expect anyone to turn up but a few did' and 'We thought that none of the students would get a job but a few did'.

fewer *see* **less**.

fiancé and **fiancée** are respectively the masculine and feminine forms of 'the person to whom one is engaged', as in 'She introduced her fiancé to her parents' and 'He gave his fiancée a magnificent engagement ring'. **Fiancé** and **fiancée** are derived from French and follow the French spelling. Note the acute accent on the *é* of **fiancé** and **fiancée** and the additional *e* on **fiancée**. Both words are pronounced in the same way—fi-*on*-say.

fictional and **fictitious** are both derived from the noun 'fiction' and are interchangeable in the sense of 'imagined, invented', as in 'a fictional character based on an old man whom he used to know' and 'The events in the novel are entirely fictitious'. However, **fictitious** only is used in the sense of 'invented, false', as in 'an entirely fictitious account of the accident' and 'think up fictitious reasons for being late'.

fill in and **fill out** are both used to mean 'to complete a form, etc, by adding the required details', as in 'fill in/ fill out an application form for a passport'. In British English **fill in** is the more common term, although **fill out** is the accepted term in American English.

finance can be pronounced in two ways. The commoner pronunciation has the emphasis on the second syllable and the first syllable pronounced like the fin of a fish (fin-*ans*). The alternative pronunciation has emphasis on the first syllable, which then is pronounced as fine (*fin*-ans). As a noun the word means 'money, capital, funding', as in 'provide the finance for the project'. As a verb it means 'to provide the money for, to pay for', as in 'expect her parents to finance her trip round the world'.

first and **firstly** are now both considered acceptable in lists, although formerly **firstly** was considered unacceptable. Originally the acceptable form of such a list was as in 'There are several reasons for staying here. First, we like the house, secondly we have pleasant neighbours, thirdly we hate moving house'. Some users now prefer to use the adjectival forms of 'second' and 'third' when using **first**, as in 'He has stated his reasons for going to another job. First, he has been offered a higher salary, second, he has more opportunities for promotion, third, he will have a company car'. As indicated, **firstly** is now quite acceptable and is the form preferred by many people, as in 'They have several reasons for not having a car. Firstly they have very little money, secondly, they live right next to the bus-stop, thirdly, they feel cars are not environmentally friendly'.

fish and **fishes** are both found as plural forms of 'fish', but **fish** is by far the more widely used form, as in 'He keeps tropical fish', 'Some fish live in fresh water and some in the sea' and 'there are now only three fish in the tank'. **Fishes** is rarely used but when it is, it is usually used to refer to different species of fish, as in 'He is comparing the fishes of the Pacific Ocean with those of the Indian Ocean'. **Fish** can also be used in this case.

first name *see* **Christian name**.

flaccid, meaning 'soft and limp', as in 'repelled by the sight of his flaccid flesh' causes problems both with reference to spelling and pronunciation. In spelling note the double *c*. As for pronunciation, **flaccid** is usually pronounced *flak*-sid but *flas*-id is a rarer alternative.

flair and **flare** are liable to be confused because they sound alike. However, they mean entirely different things. **Flair** refers to 'a natural aptitude or talent', as in 'She has a real flair for dress designing', or to 'stylishness or attractiveness', as in 'She always dresses with flair, although she does not spend much money on clothes'. As a noun, **flare** refers to a 'a bright, sudden unsteady flame', as in 'From the sea they caught sight of the flare of the bonfire on the hilltop', or 'a signal in the form of light used at sea', as in 'The captain of the sinking ship used flares to try to attract the attention of passing vessels'.

flak

As a verb **flare** means either 'to burn brightly and unsteadily', as in 'The match flared in the darkness', or 'to burst into activity', as in 'Tempers flare when the two families get together'. It also means 'to become wider at the bottom', as in 'skirts flaring at the knee'.

flak originally referred to 'gunfire aimed at enemy aircraft', as in 'Pilots returning across the English Channel encountered heavy flak'. In modern usage it is also applied to 'severe criticism', as in 'the government receiving flak for raising taxes'.

flammable and **inflammable** both mean 'easily set on fire, burning easily', as in 'Children's nightclothes should not be made of flammable/inflammable material' and 'The chemical is highly flammable/inflammable'. **Inflammable** is frequently misused because some people wrongly regard it as meaning 'not burning easily', thinking that it is like such words as 'incredible', 'inconceivable' and 'intolerant' where the prefix 'in' means 'not'.

flare *see* **flair**.

flaunt and **flout** are liable to be confused although they mean different things. **Flaunt** means 'to show off, to display in an ostentatious way', as in 'flaunting her new clothes in front of the other children who were envious of her' and 'flaunting her generous bust'. **Flout** means 'to disobey or disregard openly or scornfully', as in 'expelled for flouting school rules' and 'flout convention by not wearing evening dress'.

fleshly and **fleshy** are not interchangeable although they are both derived from the noun 'flesh'. **Fleshly** means 'referring to the body as opposed to the spirit', as in 'more

110

interested in fleshly pleasure than in prayer'. **Fleshy** means either 'soft and pulpy, as in 'ripe, fleshy peaches', or 'plump', as in 'Women with fleshy upper arms should avoid sleeveless dresses'.

flounder and **flounce** are liable to be confused although they have different meanings. **Flounder** means 'to move with difficulty or clumsily, to struggle helplessly', as in 'walkers floundering in the swampy ground' and 'to hesitate or make mistakes', as in 'The politician answered the first few questions easily but floundered when the interviewer asked him about his policies'. **Founder** means 'to sink', as in 'The ship hit some rocks and foundered' and 'to fail, to collapse', as in 'His business foundered for lack of enough capital' and 'The campaign foundered when the mayor withdrew his support'.

flout *see* **flaunt**.

flotsam and **jetsam** are often used together to refer to 'miscellaneous objects, odds and ends', as in 'We have moved most of the furniture to the new house—there's just the flotsam and jetsam left', and 'vagrants, tramps', as in 'people with no pity in their hearts for the flotsam and jetsam of society'. In the phrase **flotsam and jetsam** they are used as though they meant the same thing but this is not the case. Both words relate to the remains of a wrecked ship, but **flotsam** refers to 'the wreckage of the ship found floating in the water', as in 'The coastguards knew the ship must have broken up when they saw bits of flotsam near the rocks', while **jetsam** refers to 'goods and equipment thrown overboard from a ship in distress in order to lighten it', as in 'The coastguards

flounder

were unable to find the ship although they found the jet-sam'.

flounder *see* **founder**.

flu and **flue** are liable to be confused although they have entirely different meanings. **Flu** is a shortened form of 'influenza', as in 'He is off work with flu', 'She caught flu and had to cancel her skiing trip'. It is much more commonly used than 'influenza', which is restricted to very formal or technical contexts, as in 'an article on the dangers of influenza in a medical journal'. Note that **flu** is no longer spelt with an initial apostrophe although the spelling **'flu** was formerly common. **Flue** means 'a channel or pipe through which smoke, hot air or fumes pass from a boiler, etc, usually to a chimney', as in 'The boiler is not working properly as the flue needs to be cleaned'.

fluorescent, as in 'fluorescent lighting' or 'fluorescent paint', is frequently misspelt. Note the *uo* combination, the *sc* and *ent*.

focus as a verb has two possible spellings in its past participle and past tense. Formerly only **focused** was considered acceptable but in modern usage **focussed** is also considered acceptable. The same applies to the present participle and so **focusing** and **focussing** are both acceptable. **Focus** as a verb means 'to adjust the focus of', as in 'focus a camera'; 'to become able to see clearly', as in 'His eyes gradually began to focus in the darkened room'; 'to cause to be concentrated at a point', as in 'focus the sun's rays through a magnifying glass'; 'to concentrate (one's attention or mind) on', as in 'unable to focus his mind on the problem' and 'the committee should focus on improving the financial situation'.

As a noun **focus** has two possible plural forms. Of these **focuses** (not **focusses**) is the more common in modern usage except in very technical contexts when **foci** is used. **Focus** as a noun means 'the point at which rays of light or sound meet', as in 'the focus of the sun's rays'; 'the point at which the outline of something is most clearly seen', as in 'The trees on the horizon are not yet in focus'; 'a device or adjustment on a lens to produce a clearer image', as in 'a camera with a faulty focus'; 'centre of interest, attention, etc', as in 'The focus of the meeting was on getting the plans for the new road rejected' and 'In that dress she was the focus of attention'.

foetid *see* **fetid**.

foetus and **fetus** are both possible spellings of a word meaning 'a young human or animal that has developed within the womb but has not yet reached the stage of being born', as in 'doctors worrying about giving the pregnant woman a drug that might harm the foetus'. Originally **fetus** was restricted to American English but it is becoming increasingly used in British English also, as in 'a fetus liable to abort'. The adjective formed from **foetus/fetus** is **foetal/fetal.**

foment *see* **ferment**.

forbear and **forebear** are interchangeable in one meaning of **forbear** only. **Forbear** is a verb meaning 'to refrain from', as in 'I hope she can forbear from pointing out that she was right' and this cannot be spelt **forebear.** However, **forebear** meaning 'ancestor' can also be spelt

forbear, as in 'One of his *forebears/forbears* received a gift of land from Henry VIII'.

The verb **forbear** is pronounced with the emphasis on the second syllable as for-*bair*. The nouns **forbear** and **forebear** are pronounced alike with the emphasis on the first syllable as *for*-bair. the past tense of the verb **forbear** is **forbore**, as in 'He forbore to mention that he was responsible for the mistake'.

forever can be spelt as two words when it means 'eternally, for all time', as in 'doomed to separate forever/for ever' and 'have faith in the fact that they would dwell forever/for ever with Christ'. In the sense of 'constantly or persistently', only **forever** is used, as in 'His wife was forever nagging' and 'the child was forever asking for sweets'.

formally and **formerly** are liable to be confused because they sound alike. **Formally** means 'in a formal way', as in 'dress very formally for the dinner' and 'address the meeting formally'. **Formerly** means 'previously, before, at an earlier time', as in 'Formerly the committee used to meet twice per month' and 'He was formerly chairman of the board'.

former and **latter** are opposites. **Former** refers to 'the first of two people or things mentioned' while **latter** refers to 'the second of two people or things mentioned', as in 'He was given two options, either to stay in his present post but accept less money or to be transferred to another branch of the company. He decided to accept the former/latter option'. **Former** also means 'previous, at an earlier time', as in 'He is a former chairman of the

company' and 'She is a former holder of the champion-
ship title'.

formerly *see* **formally**.

formidable may be pronounced with the emphasis on the
first syllable as *for*-mid-ibl or with the emphasis on the
second syllable as for-*mid*-ibl. The first of these is the
more widely used. The word means 'causing fear or ap-
prehension', as in 'The sight of the raging torrent was a
formidable prospect'; 'difficult to deal with', as in 'a
formidable task'; 'arousing respect', as in 'a formidable
opponent' and 'a formidable list of qualifications'.

forte causes problems with pronunciation. The usual pronunciation in is *for*-tay but it can also be pronounced as
single syllable fort. The word means 'someone's strong
point', as in 'Putting people at their ease is not her forte'
and 'The chef's forte is desserts'. There is also a musical word **forte** meaning 'loud' or loudly'. It is of Italian
origin and is pronounced either *for*-ti or *for*-tay.

forward and **forwards** are not interchangeable in all contexts. They are interchangeable in the adverbial sense of
forward meaning 'towards the front', as in 'He took a
step forward/forwards' and 'facing forward/forwards'.
Forwards is never used as an alternative for **forward**
as an adjective, as in 'forward planning'. Nor is **forwards**
ever used in idiomatic phrasal verbs such as 'look forward', 'put forward', 'come forward', as in 'look forward to a happy retirement', 'put forward new proposals' and 'appeal to witnesses to come forward'.

founder *see* **flounder**.

foyer causes pronunciation problems. The most widely

fulfil

used pronunciation is foi-ay but it can also be pronounced fwah-yay following the original French pronunciation. It means 'an entrance hall in a hotel, theatre, etc'.

fulfil is frequently misspelt. Note that neither *l* is doubled. However the second *l* is doubled in the past tense and past participle as **fulfilled** and in the present participle as **fulfilling**. In American English the usual spelling is **fulfill**.

further *see* **farther**.

G

gaff and **gaffe** are liable to be confused because they sound alike. **Gaff** means 'a rod with an iron hook for pulling a large fish out of the water', as in 'The anglers in the boat reached for the gaff when they saw the size of the fish'. It is more commonly found in the slang phrase **blow the gaff**, meaning 'to reveal a secret', as in 'The thieves refused to tell the police where they had hidden the stolen money but the wife of one of them blew the gaff'. **Gaffe** means 'a social blunder, an indiscreet remark or deed', as in 'He wore a sports jacket to the dinner party and realized that he had made a gaffe when he saw everyone else in evening dress'.

gallop, meaning to go or ride fast, as in 'try to get the horse to gallop', is frequently misspelt. Note the double *l* and single *p*. The past tense, past participle and present participle are even more likely to be misspelt. The *p* does not double, as **galloped** and **galloping**. Thus we have 'horses which galloped across the plains' and 'watch the ponies galloping'.

gamble and **gambol** are liable to be confused because they sound alike although they mean different thing. **Gamble** is much more common than **gambol** and means 'to play games of chance for money', as in 'He gambles all night at the casino', or 'to bet, wager or risk money on

117

something uncertain', as in 'He gambled all his money on the horse in the last race' and 'He gambled all his savings on a risky business venture'. **Gambol** means 'to skip about', as in 'Lambs used to gambol in the fields here'. The single *l* doubles in the past tense, past participle and present participle as **gambolled** and **gambolling**. Thus 'The lion cubs gambolled around their mother' and 'Watch the children gambolling on the beach'.

gaol *see* **jail**.

-gate is a modern suffix which is added to a noun to indicate something scandalous. Most of the words so formed are short-lived and forgotten about almost as soon as they are invented. In modern usage they are frequently used to apply to sexual scandals, but originally **-gate** was restricted to some form of political scandal. The suffix is derived from **Watergate**, and refers to a political scandal in the United States during President Richard Nixon's re-election campaign in 1972 when Republican agents were caught breaking into the headquarters of the Democratic Party in Washington, called the Watergate Building. The uncovering of the attempts to cover up the break-in led to Richard Nixon's resignation.

gauge, meaning 'measure, standard', as in 'petrol gauge' and 'a gauge of his intelligence', is frequently misspelt. Note that the *a* comes before the *u*. It is a common error to put them the wrong way round.

gay originally meant 'merry, light-hearted', as in 'the gay laughter of children playing' and 'everyone feeling gay at the sight of the sunshine'. Although this meaning still exists in modern usage, it is rarely used since **gay** has come to be an accepted word for 'homosexual', as in 'gay rights' and 'gay bars'. Although the term can be applied to men or women it is most commonly applied to men, the corresponding word for women being **lesbian**. There is a growing tendency among homosexuals to describe themselves as **queer**, a term that was formerly regarded as being offensive.

geriatric is frequently found in medical contexts to mean 'elderly' or 'old', as in 'an ever-increasing number of geriatric patients' and 'a shortage of geriatric wards'. In such contexts **geriatric** is not used in a belittling or derogatory way, **geriatrics** being the name given to the branch of medicine concerned with the health and diseases of elderly people. However, **geriatric** is often used in the general language to refer to old people in a derogatory or scornful way, as in 'geriatric shoppers getting in the way' or 'geriatric drivers holding up the traffic'.

gibe and **jibe** both mean 'to jeer at, mock, make fun of', as in 'rich children gibing/jibing at the poor children for wearing out-of-date clothes'. **Gibe** and **jibe** are nouns as well as verbs as in 'politicians tired of the gibes/jibes of the press'.

gipsy and **gypsy** are both acceptable spellings, as in 'gipsies/gypsies travelling through the country in their caravans'. Some people object to the word **gipsy** or **gypsy**, preferring the word traveller, as in 'councils being asked to build sites for travellers'. The term **traveller** is used to apply to a wider range of people who travel the country, as in 'New Age travellers', and not just to gipsies, who are Romany in origin.

girl

girl means 'a female child or adolescent', as in 'separate schools for girls and boys' and 'Girls tend to mature more quickly than boys'. However it is often applied to a young woman, or indeed to a woman of any age, as in 'He asked his wife if she was going to have a night out with the girls from the office'. Many women object to this use, regarding it as patronizing, although the user of the term does not always intend to convey this impression.

glamorous is frequently misspelt. Note that there is no *u* before the *r*, although there is one in **glamour**. **Glamorous** means 'beautiful, stylish, elegant', as in 'glamorous filmstars'.

glutton *see* **gourmand**.

gobbledygook and **gobbledegook** are both acceptable spellings of a word meaning 'pretentious language that is difficult to understand, often found in official documents', as in 'The leaflets were meant to explain how to apply for a grant but they were written in gobbledygook'.

gorilla and **guerilla** are liable to be confused because they sound alike. They are completely different in meaning. **Gorilla** is a type of large African ape, as in 'The zoo has several gorillas'. It is also used informally to describe a large, powerful, often ugly and brutal man, as in 'The gangster has a gang of gorillas to protect him'. **Guerilla**, which can also be spelt **guerrilla**, means 'a member of an irregular army who fights in small, secret groups', as in 'The army were shot at by guerillas hiding in the hills'. Both words are pronounced alike as gir-*il*-a.

gourmand and **gourmet** and **glutton** all have reference to food but they do not mean quite the same thing. **Gour-**

mand refers to 'a person who likes food and eats a lot of it', as in 'Gourmands tucking into huge helpings of the local food'. It means much the same as **glutton**, but **glutton** is a more condemnatory term, as in 'gluttons stuffing food into their mouths'. **Gourmet** is a more refined term, being used to refer to 'a person who enjoys food and who is discriminating and knowledgeable about it', as in 'gourmets who spend their holidays seeking out good local restaurants and produce'. In modern usage **gourmet** is often used as an adjective to mean 'high-class, elaborate, expensive', as in 'gourmet restaurants' and 'gourmet foods'.

graffiti is frequently misspelt. Note the double *f* and single *t*. The word is used of 'unofficial writing and drawings, often of an obscene nature, on the walls of public places', as in 'trying to clean the graffiti from the walls of the public toilets'. Graffiti is Italian in origin and is actually the plural form of **graffito**, meaning a single piece of writing or drawing, but this is now hardly ever used in English.

gratuitous is liable to be misspelt and misunderstood. Note the *ui* combination. The word means 'uncalled-for, without good reason, unwarranted, unnecessary', as in 'resent her gratuitous advice' and 'upset by her gratuitous insults'.

gray *see* **grey**.

green is used to mean 'conserved with the conservation of the environment', as in 'a political party concerned with green issues' and 'buy as many green products as possible'. The word is derived from German *grün*, the

121

grievous

political environmental lobby having started in West Germany, as it was then called.

grievous causes problems with reference to both spelling and pronunciation. Note the *ie* combination and the absence of *i* before *ou*. It is pronounced *gree*-vus. **Grievous** means 'causing grief or suffering', as in 'grievous bodily harm', or 'serious, grave', as in 'a grievous crime'.

grey and **gray** are both acceptable spellings. In British English, however, **grey** is the more common, as in 'different shades of grey' and 'grey hair', but **gray** is the standard form in American English.

guarantee is frequently misspelt. Note the *u* before the *a* and the *a* after the *r*. It means 'a promise or assurance that certain conditions will be fulfilled', as in 'under the terms of the manufacturer's guarantee'.

guerilla, guerrilla *see* **gorilla**.

gynaecology is frequently misspelt. Note the *y* after the *g* and the *ae* combination after the *n*. **Gynaecology** refers to 'the study and treatment of disorders of women, specially of the female reproductive system', as in 'have an appointment at the gynaecology department'. The American English spelling is **gynecology**.

gypsy *see* **gipsy**.

H

haemorrhage is frequently misspelt. Note the *ae* and the *rrh* combinations. It can be either a noun meaning 'excessive loss of blood', as in 'a haemorrhage from the womb after the birth of the baby', or a verb meaning 'to bleed heavily', as in 'haemorrhaging badly after the birth of the baby'. In American English the word is spelt **hemorrhage**.

hail and **hale** are liable to be confused. They are pronounced alike but have different meanings. **Hail** refers to frozen rain, as in 'get caught in a storm of hail', or to 'something coming in great numbers and with force', as in 'a hail of bullets'. As a verb it means 'to fall as hail', as in 'It began to hail', or 'to come down fast and with force', as in 'Bullets hailed down on them'. There is another word **hail**, which is a verb that means 'to call to in order to attract attention', as in 'He hailed a friend on the other side of the street'; 'to acknowledge enthusiastically as in 'hail him as their new leader' and 'hail his new painting as a masterpiece'; 'to come from', as in 'She hails from a small town up north'. **Hale** means 'healthy and strong' and is frequently found in the phrase 'hale and hearty', as in 'he was very ill but he is hale and hearty again'.

hallo, hello and **hullo** are all acceptable spellings of a word

handicap

used in greeting, as in 'Hallo/hello/hullo, I didn't expect
to see you here' and 'He was in a hurry and didn't stop
to say "hallo/hello/hullo"'.

handicap is frequently misspelt in the past tense, past
participle and present participle, as in 'physically handicapped people' and 'handicapping circumstances'. The
word **handicap** is disliked by some people because they
feel it is too negative a term. There is as yet no wide-
spread alternative apart from **disabled**, although various suggestions have been made as part of the politically correct language movement, such as **physically challenged** and **differently abled**.

hangar and **hanger** are liable to be confused since they
sound alike. However, they have totally different meanings. **Hangar** refers to 'a building for housing aircraft',
as in 'a hangar holding four small aircraft'. **Hanger** refers to 'an apparatus on which clothes are hung', as in
'The hotel didn't provide enough hangars for their
clothes'.

hanged and **hung** are both past participles and past tenses
of the verb 'to hang' but they are used in different contexts. **Hanged** is restricted to the sense of 'hang' that
means 'to suspend by the neck until dead', as in 'He was
hanged for murder' and 'She hanged herself while de-
pressed'. **Hung** is used in the other sense of 'hang', as
in 'They hung the picture on the wall by the door' and
'A towel hung from the rail'.

hanger *see* **hangar**.

harass causes problems with reference both to spelling
and pronunciation. Note the single *r* and the double *s*. It

is a common error to put double *r* and single *s*. There are two possible pronunciations. Traditionally it is pronounced with the stress on the first syllable, as *har*-as. However, in modern usage there is an increasing tendency to put the emphasis on the second syllable, as har-*as*, which is how the word is pronounced in America.

hard and **soft** are both terms applied to drugs. **Hard drugs** refer to 'strong drugs that are likely to be addictive', as in 'Heroin and cocaine are hard drugs'. **Soft drugs** refer to 'drugs that are considered unlikely to cause addiction', as in 'cannabis and other soft drugs'.

hardly is used to indicate a negative idea. Therefore a sentence or clause containing it does not require another negative. Sentences, such as 'I couldn't hardly see him' and 'He left without hardly a word' are *wrong*. They should read 'I could hardly see him' and 'He left with hardly a word'. **Hardly** is followed by 'when', not 'than', as in 'Hardly had he entered the house when he collapsed', although the 'than' construction is very common.

hare-brained is frequently misspelt as 'hair-brained'. It means 'foolish', as in 'a hare-brained scheme to make money'.

height is a simple word that is frequently misspelt. Note the *ei* and the *gh* combination. As well as meaning 'the distance from the bottom to the top of a person or object', as in 'measure the child's height', it can mean 'the highest point of something', as in 'at the height of his career', or 'the most intense or extreme point of something', as in 'at the height of their passion'.

heinous

heinous, meaning 'very wicked', as in 'a heinous crime', causes problems both with reference to spelling and pronunciation. Note the *ei*. It is most commonly pronounced *hay*-nis, although *hee*-nis also exists.

hello *see* **hallo.**

he/she is a convention used to avoid sexism. Before the rise of feminism anyone referred to, whose sex was not specified, was assumed to be male, as in 'Each pupil must take his book home' and 'Every driver there parked his car illegally'. The only exception to this occurred in situations that were thought to be particularly appropriate to women, as in 'The cook should make her own stock' and 'The nurse has left her book behind'. In modern usage where attempts are made to avoid sexism either **he/she** or 'he or she' is frequently used, as in 'Each manager is responsible for his/her department' or 'It is a doctor's duty to explain the nature of the treatment to his or her patient'. People who regard this convention as being clumsy should consider restructuring the sentence or putting it in the plural, as in 'All managers are responsible for their departments'. Some users prefer to be ungrammatical and use a plural pronoun with a singular noun, as in 'Every pupil should take their books home'.

hereditary and **heredity** are liable to be confused. **Hereditary** is an adjective meaning 'passed on from parent to child, genetically transmitted', as in 'suffer from a hereditary disease', or 'passed on from parent to child, inherited', as in 'a hereditary title'. **Heredity** is the noun from which **hereditary** is derived, as in 'part of his genetic heredity' and 'The disease can be put down to heredity'.

heterosexism refers to 'discrimination and prejudice by a heterosexual person against a homosexual one', as in 'He was convinced that he had not got the job because he was gay—that the employer had been guilty of heterosexism'.

historic and **historical** are both adjectives formed from the noun history' but they are not interchangeable. **Historic** refers to events that are important enough to earn, or have earned, a place in history, as in 'Nelson's historic victory at Trafalgar' and 'the astronaut's historic landing on the moon'. It can be used loosely to mean 'extremely memorable', as in 'attend a historic party'. **Historical** means 'concerning past events', as in 'historical studies', or 'based on the study of history, as in 'take into consideration only historical facts' and 'produce historical evidence'.

hoard and **horde** are liable to be confused. They sound alike but they have completely different meanings. **Hoard** refers to 'a collected and reserved store', as in 'the miser's hoard of money' and 'a hoard of old comics'. It can also be a verb meaning 'to collect and store', as in 'hoarding food because they thought it was going to be rationed' and 'squirrels hoarding nuts for the winter'. **Horde** refers to 'a large crowd of people, a multitude', as in 'Hordes of people arrived to see the pop star arriving at the theatre'.

honorary and **honourable** are liable to be confused. They are both derived from the noun **honour**, but they mean

hopefully

different things. **Honorary** means 'given as an honour
rather than acquired through the usual channels', as in
'an honorary degree', or 'unpaid', as in 'the honorary
secretary' and 'an honorary post'. **Honourable** means
'showing honour', as in 'an honourable man' and 'the
honourable thing to do', and 'worthy of honour', as in
'perform honourable deeds in battle'.

hopefully has two meanings. The older meaning is 'with
hope', as in 'The child looked hopefully at the sweet-
shop window' and 'It is better to travel hopefully than to
arrive'. A more recent meaning, which is disliked by
some people, means 'it is to be hoped that', as in 'Hopefully we shall soon be there'.

horde *see* **hoard**.

hospitable can be pronounced in two ways. The more traditional pronunciation has the emphasis on the first syllable, as *hos*-pit-ibl. In modern usage it is sometimes
pronounced with the emphasis on the second syllable,
as hos-*pit*-ibl. The word means 'showing or giving hos-
pitality, generous to guests', as in 'He is very hospitable
and is always having people to stay' and 'a most hospitable hostess who fed her guests very well'.

hullo *see* **hallo**.

human and **humane** are liable to be confused. **Human**
means either 'referring to human beings', as in 'not fit
for human habitation', or 'kindly', as in 'He holds a very
important position but he is a very human person'. **Humane** means 'showing kindness, sympathy or understanding', as in 'their humane attitude to prisoners of
war' and 'Be humane and put the dying animal to sleep'.

128

humanism and **humanitarianism** are liable to be confused. **Humanism** is a philosophy that values greatly human beings and their rôle, and rejects the need for religion, as in 'She was brought up as a Christian but she decided to embrace humanism in later life'. **Humanitarianism** refers to the philosophy and actions of people who wish to improve the lot of their fellow human beings and help them, as in 'humanitarians trying to help the refugees by taking them food and clothes'.

humorous is frequently misspelt. Note the *o* before the *r*. It is liable to be confused with 'humour' and an extra *u* added before the *r*.

hung *see* **hanged**.

hygiene is liable to be misspelt. Note the *y* after the *h*, not *i*. It means 'the study and practice of cleanliness and good health', as in 'poor standards of hygiene in the hotel kitchens'.

hyper- and **hypo-** are liable to be confused. They sound rather similar but they are opposites. **Hyper-** means 'above, excessively', as in 'hyperactive', 'hyperexcitable'. **Hypo-** means 'under, beneath', as in 'hypothermia'.

I

-ible *see* **-able**.

identical in modern usage can be followed by either 'with' or 'to'. Formerly only 'with' was considered correct, as in 'His new suit is identical with the one he bought last year'. Now 'to' is also considered acceptable, as in 'a brooch identical to one which he bought for his wife'.

idioms are expressions the meanings of which are different from the literal meanings of the individual words that they contain. Thus 'straight from the shoulder', 'have a finger in every pie' and 'have one's back to the wall' are all idioms.

idiosyncrasy is frequently misspelt. Note the *y* after the *s*, and the *asy* combination, not *acy*. It means 'a particular and individual way of behaving, thinking, etc', as in 'It was one of his idiosyncrasies always to buy yellow cars'.

idle and **idol** are liable to be confused since they sound alike. They mean entirely different things. **Idle** is an adjective meaning 'inactive, not functioning', as in 'machines lying idle', and 'lazy', as in 'too idle to get up and do any work'. **Idol** refers to 'something or someone that one worships or admires', as in 'worship idols carved from wood', 'Her elder brother was her idol' and 'pop stars who are the idols of teenagers'.

idyllic causes problems both with reference to spelling and pronunciation. Note the *y* and double *l*. It is pronounced with the emphasis on the second syllable and the first syllable is usually pronounced to rhyme with 'lid', as in id-*il*-ik. The first syllable is sometimes pronounced with 'wide', as in *id*-il-ik. The word means 'peaceful and pleasant, perfect', as in 'a cottage in an idyllic setting'.

i.e. is the abbreviation of a Latin phrase *id est*, meaning 'that is', as in 'He is a lexicographer, i.e. a person who edits dictionaries'. It is mostly used in written, rather than formal contexts.

illegible and **eligible** are liable to be confused although they have completely different meanings. **Illegible** means 'impossible to decipher, make out or read', as in 'unable to understand the message because of her totally illegible handwriting'. **Eligible** means 'qualified, suitable', as in 'several candidates who were eligible for the post' and 'eligible bachelors'. **Illegible** is pronounced with the emphasis on the the second syllable (il-*lej*-ibl) but **eligible** is pronounced with the emphasis on the first syllable (*el*-ij-ibl).

illegible and **unreadable** are not totally interchangeable. **Illegible** refers to something that is impossible to make out or decipher, as in 'her handwriting is practically illegible'. **Unreadable** can also mean this, as in 'unreadable handwriting', but it can also mean 'unable to be read with understanding or enjoyment', as in 'His writing is so full of jargon that it is unreadable'.

illicit and **elicit** are liable to be confused. They sound alike although they have totally different meanings. **Illicit** means 'unlawful', as in 'the sale of illicit drugs', or

illusion

'against the rules of society', as in 'His wife did not
know about his illicit affair with his secretary'. **Elicit**
means 'to draw out, often with difficulty', as in 'We
finally succeeded in eliciting a response from them' and
'All attempts at eliciting the truth from the boy failed'.
Both words sound alike, with the emphasis on the second syllable as il-*lis*-it.

illusion *see* **allusion**.

illusion *see* **delusion**.

imaginary and **imaginative** are liable to be confused.
They are related but do not mean the same thing. **Imaginary** means 'existing only in the imagination, unreal',
as in 'The child has an imaginary friend'. **Imaginative**
means 'having a vivid or creative imagination', as in
'An imaginative child who was always inventing her
own games', and 'indicating or using a vivid or creative
imagination', as in 'an imaginative adventure story'.

imbroglio means 'a confused, complicated or embarrassing situation', as in 'politicians getting involved in an
international imbroglio during the summit conference'.
It is liable to be misspelt and mispronounced. Note the
g which is liable to be omitted erroneously as it is not
pronounced. It is pronounced im-*bro*-lio with emphasis
on the second syllable which rhymes with 'foe'. **Imbroglio** is used only in formal or literary contexts.

immigrant *see* **emigrant**.

immoral *see* **amoral**.

impasse causes problems with reference to meaning, spelling and pronunciation. It means 'a difficult position or
situation from which there is no way out, deadlock', as

in 'The negotiations between management and workers have reached an impasse with neither side being willing to compromise'. Note the final *e* in the spelling. The first syllable can be pronounced 'am', or 'om' in an attempt at following the original French pronunciation, although in modern usage it is frequently totally anglicized as 'im'.

impeccable is frequently misspelt. Note the *-able*, not *-ible*, and the double *c*. The word means 'faultless, free from error or defect', as in 'The pianist gave an impeccable performance' and 'It was a difficult situation but his behaviour was impeccable'.

impious is frequently misspelt. The emphasis should be on the first syllable as *im*-pi-us. This is unlike 'impiety' where the stress is on the second syllable. **Impious** means 'showing a lack of respect for God or religion'.

implicit *see* **explicit**.

imply and **infer** are often used interchangeably but they in fact are different in meaning. **Imply** means 'to suggest, to hint at', as in 'We felt that she was implying that he was lying' and 'She did not actually say that there was going to be a delay but she implied it'. **Infer** means 'to deduce, to conclude', as in 'From what the employer said we inferred that there would be some redundancies' and 'From the annual financial reports observers inferred the company was about to go bankrupt'. Note that **infer** doubles the *r* when adding '-ed' or '-ing' to form the past tense, past participle or present participle as **inferred** and **inferring**.

impracticable and **impractical** are liable to be confused.

inapt

Impracticable means 'impossible to put into practice, not workable', as in 'In theory the plan is fine but it is impracticable in terms of costs'. **Impractical** means 'not sensible or realistic', as in 'It is impractical to think that you will get there and back in a day'; 'not skilled at doing or making things', as in 'He is a brilliant academic but he is hopelessly impractical'.

inapt and **inept** are similar in meaning in one sense of **inept**. **Inapt** means 'inappropriate, unsuitable', as in 'The speaker's remarks were totally inapt', 'make a few inapt comments on the situation' and 'inapt behaviour'. **Inept** can mean much the same as this except that it suggests also clumsiness', as in 'embarrassed by his inept remarks'. **Inept** also means 'unskilful, clumsy', as in 'his inept handling of the situation' and 'make an inept attempt at mending the roof'.

incomparable is liable to be mispronounced. The emphasis should be on the second syllable and not the third. It should be pronounced in-*kom*-pir-ibl. **Incomparable** means 'without compare', as in 'her incomparable kindness' and in 'his incomparable rendition of the song'.

incredible and **incredulous** are liable to be confused although they mean different things. **Incredible** means 'unbelievable' or 'difficult to believe', as in 'I find his account of the accident totally incredible' and 'It is incredible that everyone accepts his story'. It also means 'amazing', as in 'earn an incredible amount of money'. **Incredulous** means 'not believing, disbelieving', as in 'His incredulous listeners stared at him'.

indefinite article *see* **a**.

indefinitely is frequently misspelt. Note the *i* before the *t*. Many people wrongly put an *a*. It means 'for an unspecified time', as in 'You could wait indefinitely for a car exactly like that'.

independent is frequently misspelt. Note the final *e*. It is never spelt with an *a*. *See* **dependant**.

indexes and **indices** are both plural forms of 'index'. In modern usage **indexes** is the more common form in general language, as in 'Indexes are essential in large reference books'. An **index** in this sense is 'an alphabetical list given at the back of a book as a guide to its contents'. The form **indices** is mostly restricted to technical contexts, such as mathematical information. **Indices** is pronounced in-dis-is and is the Latin form of the plural.

indict and **indite** are liable to be confused since they are pronounced alike but they have different meanings. **Indict** means 'to charge, to accuse', as in 'He has been indicted on a charge of murder'. **Indite** is a rarer word meaning 'to write down', as in 'The headmaster indited the names of the culprits on an official report'. The words are both pronounced with the emphasis on the second syllable which rhymes with 'light' as in-*dit*.

indispensable is frequently misspelt. Note the *-able* ending, not *-ible*. It means 'absolutely essential', as in 'He now finds his computer indispensable' and 'Since both parents work full time a good nanny is indispensable'.

indite *see* **indict**.

individual refers to 'a single person as opposed to a group', as in 'The rights of the community matter but so do the rights of the individual'. **Individual** is also sometimes

indoor

used instead of 'person', but in such cases it is often used in a disapproving or belittling way, as in 'What an unpleasant individual she is!' and 'The individual who designed that building should be shot'.

indoor and **indoors** are not interchangeable. **Indoor** is an adjective, as in 'have an indoor match' and 'indoor games'. **Indoors** is an adverb, as in 'children playing outdoors instead of watching television indoors' and 'sleep outdoors on warm evenings instead of indoors'.

inequality and **inequity** are liable to be confused although they mean different things. **Inequality** means 'lack of equality, the state of being unequal or different', as in 'an inequality in the pay structures of the male and female workers' and 'fight against racial inequalities in the job market'. **Inequity** means 'unfairness, unjustness', as in 'feel that there was a certain inequity in the judge's decision'.

infectious *see* **contagious**.

infer *see* **imply**.

infinite and **infinitesimal** are similar in meaning but are not interchangeable. **Infinite** means 'without limit', as in 'infinite space', or 'very great', as in 'have infinite patience' and 'He seems to have an infinite capacity for hard work'. **Infinitesimal** means 'very small, negligible', as in 'an infinitesimal difference in size' and 'an infinitesimal increase'. **Infinitesimal** is pronounced with the emphasis on the fourth syllable in-fin-it-*es*-im-il.

inflammable *see* **flammable**.

influenza *see* **flu**.

informer and **informant** both refer to 'a person who pro-

136

vides information' but they are used in different contexts. **Informer** is used to refer to 'a person who gives information to the police or authorities about a criminal, fugitive, etc', as in 'The local police have a group of informers who tell them what is going on in the criminal underworld' and 'The resistance worker was caught by the enemy soldier when an informer told them about his activities'. An **informant** provides more general information, as in 'My informant keeps me up-to-date with changes in personnel'.

ingenious and **ingenuous** are liable to be confused. They look rather alike but they mean completely different things. **Ingenious** means 'clever, inventive', as in 'an ingenious device for opening wine bottles' and 'It was ingenious of her to find a quick way to get to the new house'. **Ingenuous** means 'innocent' or 'naive', as in 'so ingenuous as to believe his lies'.

in-law is usually found in compounds such as 'mother-in-law' and 'father-in-law'. When these compounds are in the plural the *s* should be added to the first word of the compound, not to **in-law**, as in 'mothers-in-law' and 'fathers-in-law'.

in lieu, which means 'instead of', as in 'receive extra pay in lieu of holidays', causes problems with pronunciation. It may be pronounced in lew or in loo.

innocuous is frequently misspelt. Note the double *n* and the *ouo* combination. It means 'harmless', as in 'He has a reputation for fierceness but he seems fairly innocuous' and 'It seemed an innocuous remark but she was upset by it'.

input

input used to be a technical term with particular application to computers. This meaning still exists and **input** can refer to the data, power, etc, put into a computer. As a verb it means 'to enter data into a computer', as in 'input the details of all the travel resorts in the area'. In modern usage it is frequently used in general language to mean 'contribution', as in 'Everyone is expected to provide some input for tomorrow's conference'. It is even found in this sense as a verb, as in 'input a great deal to the meeting'.

inquiry *see* **enquiry**.

install and **instal** are now both considered acceptable spellings. **Install** was formerly considered to be the only correct spelling and it is still the more common. The *l* is doubled in **instal** in the past participle, past tense and present participle as **installed**, **installing**. It means 'to put in', as in 'he installed a new television set'. The noun is spelt **instalment**.

instantaneously and **instantly** are interchangeable. Both mean 'immediately, at once', as in 'They obeyed instantaneously/instantly' and 'The accident victims were killed instantly/instantaneously'.

instil is often misspelt 'instill'. Note the single *l*. It means 'to introduce gradually', as in 'instil a sense of responsibility into children'. The *l* doubles in the past participle, past tense and present participle as **instilled** and **instilling**.

intense and **intensive** are not interchangeable. Intense means 'very strong, extreme', as in 'an intense desire to scream' and 'unable to tolerate the intense cold on the

138

icy slopes'. **Intensive** means 'thorough', as in 'conduct an intensive search', and 'concentrated', as in 'an intensive course in first aid' and 'intensive bombing'.

interment and **internment** mean different things. **Interment** means 'burial', as in 'delay the interment of the bodies until a post mortem takes place'. **Internment** means 'imprisonment, especially of prisoners-of-war, etc', as in 'released at the end of the war after several years of internment'. In both **interment** and **internment** the emphasis is on the second syllable.

interpretative and **interpretive** are both forms of the same word. They mean 'interpreting', as in 'an interpretative/ interpretive study of his poetry'.

introvert *see* **extrovert**.

invalid refers to two different words. If it is pronounced with the emphasis on the second syllable, as in-*val*-id it means 'not valid, no longer valid', as in 'This visa becomes invalid after six months'. If it is pronounced with the emphasis on the first syllable, as *in*-val-id, it means 'a person who is ill', as in 'The doctor has arrived to see the invalid'.

invent *see* **discover**.

inventory is liable to be pronounced wrongly. Unlike the word 'invention', the emphasis is on the first syllable as *in*-ven-tri or *in*-ven-tor-i. **Inventory** means 'a detailed list of goods in a house, etc,' as in 'Take an inventory of the furniture before you rent the house'.

inward and **inwards** are not used interchangeably. **Inward** is an adjective, as in 'an inward curve' and 'No one could guess her inward feelings'. **Inwards** is an adverb, as in 'toes turning inwards' and 'thoughts turning inwards'. **Inward** can be used as an adverb in the same way as **inwards.**

IQ is the abbreviation of 'intelligence quotient', as in 'He has a high IQ. It is always written in capital letters and is sometimes written with full stops and sometimes not, according to preference.

irascible is frequently misspelt. Unlike 'irritable' it has a single *r*. Note the *c* and the *-ible* ending. It means 'easily roused to anger', as in 'The children were told not to disturb the irascible old man'.

irony is 'the expression of one's meaning by saying the direct opposite of one's thoughts', as in 'This is a fine state of affairs' when in fact things have gone wrong. The adjective is **ironic**, as in 'make ironic remarks'.

irrelevant is frequently misspelt. Note the double r and the *-ant* ending.

irreparable is frequently both mispronounced and misspelt. Note the double *r*, the *a* before the *r* and the *-able* ending. It should be pronounced with the emphasis on the second syllable, as ir-*rep*-ar-abl. The word means 'unable to be put right', as in 'Being abused as a child inflicted irreparable mental damage on him'. It is usually applied to abstract nouns, **unrepairable** being used for objects, as in 'shoes that are unrepairable'. **Unrepairable** is pronounced with the emphasis on the third syllable (*pair*) which rhymes with 'care'.

irrespective is followed by the preposition 'of'. The phrase means 'not taking account of, not taking into consideration', as in 'All can go on the trip, irrespective of age'.

irrevocable is frequently misspelt and mispronounced. Note the double *r* and the *-able* ending. It is pronounced with the emphasis on the second syllable, as ir-*rev*-ok-ibl. When applied to legal judgements, etc, it is sometimes pronounced with the emphasis on the third syllable, as ir-rev-*ok*-ibl. The word means 'unable to be changed or revoked', as in 'Their decision to get divorced is irrevocable' and 'The jury's decision is irrevocable'.

-ise and **-ize** are both verb endings. In British English there are many verbs that can be spelt ending in either **-ise** or **-ize**, as 'computerise/ize', 'economise/ize', 'finalise/ize', 'hospitalise/ize', 'modernise/ize', 'organise/ize', 'realise/ize', 'theorise/ize'. There are a few verbs that cannot be spelt **-ize**. These include 'advertise', 'advise', 'comprise', 'despise', 'exercise', 'revise', 'supervise' and 'televise'.

-ism is a suffix originally used to form nouns indicating doctrine or system, as in 'Thatcherism' and 'Marxism'. This use is still current but **-ism** is now commonly used to indicate discrimination, as in 'ageism', 'racism', 'sexism'. The agent nouns from nouns ending in **-ism** in the latter sense end in **-ist**, as 'ageist', 'racist', 'sexist'.

itinerary is frequently misspelt. Note the *e* before the first *r*, and the *a* before the second *r*.

its and **it's** are liable to be confused. **Its** is an adjective meaning 'belonging to it', as in 'The house has lost its charm' and 'The dog does not like its kennel'. **It's** means 'it is', as in 'Do you know if it's raining?' and 'It's not fair to expect her to do all the chores'.

-ize *see* **-ise**.

J

jail and **gaol** are both acceptable spellings although jail is the more common. They mean 'prison' and can be both nouns and verbs, as in 'sent to jail/gaol for killing his wife' and 'jail/gaol him for his part in the bank robbery'.

jargon refers to the technical or specialized language used by a particular group, e.g. doctors, computer engineers, sociologists, etc, to communicate with each other within their specialty. It should be avoided in the general language as it will not be clear to the ordinary person exactly what is meant.

jersey *see* **cardigan**.

jeopardize is liable to be misspelt. Note the *o*. It is pronounced *jep*-er-dise and means 'to put at risk', as in 'He jeopardizes his career by his unpunctuality.'

jetsam *see* **flotsam**.

jettison is frequently misspelt. Note the double *t* and single *s*. In the past tense, past participle and present participle the *n* is not doubled, as **jettisoned** and **jettisoning**. It means 'to throw out, especially in order to make a ship, aircraft, etc, lighter', as in 'The ship's captain decided to jettison most of the cargo'. It also means 'to abandon, reject', as in 'They have had to jettison their plans for expansion because of lack of money'.

jewellery and **jewelry** are both acceptable spellings, as in

142

'A great deal of jewellery/jewelry was stolen in the robbery', but **jewellery** is the more common spelling in British English.

jibe *see* **gibe**.

jodhpurs, meaning 'trousers worn when horse-riding', is frequently misspelt. Note the *h*, which is liable to be omitted since it is silent, or put in the wrong place. The word is pronounced *jod*-purs.

judgement and **judgment** are both acceptable spellings, as in 'accept the judgement/judgment of the referee', although in British English **judgement** is slightly more common. **Judgment** is used in legal contexts.

judicial and **judicious** are liable to be confused but they are completely different in meaning. **Judicial** means 'referring to a court of law', as in 'judicial proceedings' and 'a judicial inquiry'. **Judicious** means 'having or showing good sense or judgement, wise', as in ' a judicious choice of words' and 'a judicious course of action'.

just is liable to be put in the wrong place in a sentence. It should be placed before the word it refers to, as in 'He has just one book left to sell', not 'He just has one book left to sell'. **Just** in the sense of 'in the very recent past' is used with the perfect tense, as in 'They have just finished the job', not 'They just finished the job'.

K

kaleidoscope is frequently misspelt. Note the *ei* and the first *o*. It is pronounced with the emphasis on the second syllable, which rhymes with 'my', as kal-*i*-do-skop. **Kaleidoscope** refers to 'a kind of toy consisting of a tube containing small loose pieces of coloured glass and mirrors which reflect the glass pieces to form changing patterns when the tube is turned', as in 'The child was fascinated by the changing colours of the kaleidoscope'. It also means 'a constantly and rapidly changing pattern', as in 'The Eastern market was a kaleidoscope of colour', or 'a succession of changing phases', as in 'the kaleidoscope of international politics'.

kerb *see* **curb**.

khaki is frequently misspelt. Note the *h* after the first *k*. It is liable either to be omitted in error or put in the wrong place. **Khaki** is pronounced kah-ki and refers to 'a yellowish brown colour', as in 'Military uniforms are often khaki in colour'.

kidnap is liable to be misspelt in the past tense, past participle and present participle when it doubles the *p* as **kidnapped, kidnapping.** The agent noun, 'one who kidnaps', is spelt **kidnapper. Kidnap** means 'to take away by force and illegally, often with a view to obtaining money or having specified demands met', as in 'The president's daughter was kidnapped by a gang who asked her father for a huge ransom' and 'The terrorists kidnapped the foreign diplomat and would not let him go unless some of their number were released from prison in his country'.

kilometre has two possible pronunciations in modern usage. It can be pronounced with the emphasis on the first syllable, as *kil*-o-meet-er, or with the emphasis on the second syllable, as kil-*om*-it-er. The first of these is the more traditional pronunciation but the second is becoming common. The word means 'the metric unit of length', as in 'It is 200 kilometres from there to Paris'.

kind should be used with a singular noun, as 'This kind of accident can be avoided'. This should not read 'These kind of accidents can be avoided'. Similarly 'The children do not like that kind of film' is correct, not 'The children do not like those kind of films'. A plural noun can be used if the sentence is rephrased as 'Films of that kind are not liked by children'.

   Kind of, meaning 'rather', as in 'That restaurant's kind of dear' and 'She's kind of tired of him', is informal and should be avoided in formal contexts.

kindly can be either an adjective or adverb. The adjective means 'kind, friendly, sympathetic', as in 'A kindly lady took pity on the children and lent them some money to get home' and 'She gave them a kindly smile'. The adverb means 'in a kind manner', as in 'We were treated kindly by the local people' and 'They will not look kindly on his actions'.

kneeled and **knelt**, the past tense and past participle of

knit

the verb 'to kneel', are both acceptable spellings although **knelt** is more common, as in 'He knelt and asked for forgiveness' and 'She knelt down to look under the car'.

knit in modern usage is becoming increasingly used as a noun to mean 'a knitted garment', as in 'a shop selling beautifully coloured knits'.

knowledgeable is frequently misspelt. Note the *d*, which is often omitted in error, the *e* after the *g*, which is also liable to be omitted in error, and the *-able* ending. **Knowledgeable** means 'knowing a lot, well-informed', as in 'take advice from people more knowledgeable than himself' and 'He is extremely knowledgeable on the subject of ancient Greece'.

L

laboratory is frequently mispronounced. It should be pronounced with the emphasis on the second syllable, as lab-*or*-a-tor-i or lab-*or*-a-tri. In American English the emphasis is on the first syllable. The word refers to a 'room or building where scientific work, such as research and experiments, is carried out', as in 'collect the results of the blood tests from the laboratory'.

laborious is frequently misspelt. Note that there is no *u* before *r*. It is not spelt like 'labour'. It means 'needing much effort', as in 'It was a laborious task to move all the books from the attic', or 'showing signs of effort, not fluent or flowing', as in 'His laborious style of prose is difficult to read'.

labyrinth is liable to be misspelt. Note the *y* before the *r* and the *i* after *r*. It means 'a network of winding paths, passages, etc, through which it is difficult to find one's way', as in 'a labyrinth of underground passages underneath the castle' and 'unable to find one's way around the labyrinth of regulations'.

lady and **woman** cause controversy. **Lady** is objected to by many people when it is used instead of **woman**. Formerly, and still in some circles, it was regarded as a polite form of **woman**, as in '"Please get up and give that lady a seat", said the mother to her son'. Indeed, **wom-**

laid

an was thought to be rather insulting. For many people **woman** is now the preferred term and **lady** is seen as classist, because it is associated with nobility, privilege, etc, or condescending. However, **lady** is still quite commonly used, particularly when women are being addressed in a group, as in '"Ladies, I hope we can reach our sales target", said the manager' and 'Come along, ladies the bus is about to leave'. Phrases, such as **dinner lady** and **cleaning lady** are thought by some to be condescending but others still find **woman** rather insulting.

laid and **lain** are liable to be confused. **Laid** is the past participle and past tense of **lay**, 'to put, place', as in 'They have laid a new carpet in the dining room' and 'We laid the blanket on the ground'. **Lain** is the past participle of **lie**, 'to rest in a horizontal position', as in 'He had lain there for hours before they found him'. *See* also **lay**.

lama and **llama** are liable to be confused although they have completely different meanings. **Llama** means 'a kind of South American animal', as in 'go to see the llama enclosure in the zoo'. **Lama** refers to a monk who is member of the order of Lamaism, a form of Buddhism in Tibet and Mongolia, as in 'lamas gathering for prayer'.

lamentable is frequently mispronounced. It should be pronounced with the emphasis on the first syllable, as *lam-en-tabl*. However it is becoming common to place the emphasis on the second syllable in the same way that 'lament' does. It means 'deplorable, regrettable', as in 'showing a lamentable lack of consideration for other people's feelings'.

languor is frequently misspelt. Note the *uo* combination and note that there is not a *u* before the *r*. It means 'weariness, listlessness, laziness', as in 'people full of languor on that hot, still afternoon'. The adjective from **languor** is **languorous**, as in 'feeling languorous after drinking so much wine at lunch'.

last is liable to cause confusion because it is not always clear which meaning is meant. **Last** as an adjective has several meanings. It can mean 'final', as in 'That was the musician's last public appearance—he died shortly after'; 'coming after all others in time or order', as in 'December is the last month in the year', 'The last of the runners reached the finishing tape'; 'latest, most recent', as in 'Her last novel is not as good as her earlier ones'; 'previous, preceding', as in 'This chapter is interesting but the last one was boring'. In order to avoid confusion it is best to use a word other than **last** where ambiguity is likely to arise. An example of a sentence which could cause confusion is 'I cannot remember the title of his last book', which could mean either 'his latest book' or 'his final book'.

latter *see* **former**.

lavatory *see* **toilet**.

lay and **lie** are liable to be confused. They are related but are used in different contexts. **Lay** means 'to put or place' and is a transitive verb, i.e. it takes an object. It is found in such sentences as 'Ask them to lay the books carefully on the table' and 'They are going to lay a new carpet in the bedroom'. **Lie**, meaning 'to rest in a horizontal position', is an intransitive verb, i.e. it does not take an object. It is found in such sentences as 'They were told

lead

to lie on the ground' and 'Snow is apt to lie on the mountain tops for a long time'. The confusion between the two words arises from the fact that **lay** is also the past tense of **lie**, as in 'He lay still on the ground' and 'Snow lay on the mountain tops'. The past tense of **lay** is **laid**, as in 'They laid the books on the table'. There is another verb **lie**, meaning 'to tell falsehoods, not to tell the truth', as in 'He was told to lie to the police'. The past tense of **lie** in this sense is **lied**, as in 'We suspect that he lied but we cannot prove it'. *See also* **laid**.

lead and **led** are liable to be confused. **Lead**, pronounced to rhyme with 'feed', is a verb meaning 'to guide, to show the way to, especially by going in front of', as in 'He lead the police to the spot where he had found the murdered man'. **Lead**, pronounced to rhyme with 'fed, means 'a kind of metal', as in 'replace water pipes made of lead'. **Led**, which also rhymes with fed, is thus pronounced in the same way as **lead** in the sense of metal. It is the past participle and past tense of the verb **lead**, as in 'He had led the search party to the wrong place' and 'The guide led the climbers to the top of the mountain'.

leading question is often used wrongly. It should be used to mean 'a question that is so worded as to invite (or lead to) a particular answer desired by the questioner', as in 'The judge refused to allow the barrister to ask the witness the question on the grounds that it was a leading question'. However, it is often used wrongly to mean 'a question that is difficult, unfair or embarrassing'.

leaned and **leant** are both acceptable forms of the past participle and past tense of the verb 'to lean', as in 'He

had *leaned/leant* the ladder against the garage wall' and
he *leaned/leant* on the gate and watched the cows'.
Leaned is pronounced leend or lent, and **leant** is pronounced lent.

leaped and **leapt** are both acceptable forms of the past
participle and past tense of the verb 'to leap', as in 'He
leaped /leapt to his feet and shouted out' and 'The dog
had *leaped/leapt* over the fence'. **Leaped** is pronounced
either leept or leapt, and **leapt** is pronounced lept.

learn and **teach** are liable to be confused. **Learn** means
'to gain information or knowledge about', as in 'She
learnt Spanish as a child', or 'to gain the skill of', as in
'She is learning to drive'. **Teach** means 'to give instruction in, to cause to know something or be able to do
something', as in 'She taught her son French' and 'She
taught her son to swim'. **Learn** is frequently used wrongly instead of **teach**, as in 'She learnt us to drive'.

learned and **learnt** are both acceptable forms of the past
participle and past tense of the verb 'to learn', as in 'She
has now *learned/learnt* to drive' and 'They *learned/
learnt* French at school'. **Learned** in this sense can be
pronounced either lernd or leant. However, **learned** can
also be an adjective, meaning 'having much knowledge,
erudite', as in 'an learned professor', or 'academic', as
in 'learned journals'. It is pronounced *ler*-ned.

leave and **let** are not interchangeable. **Leave go** should
not be substituted for **let go** in such sentences as 'Do not
let go of the rope'. 'Do not leave go of the rope' is considered to be incorrect. However both **leave alone** and
let alone can be used in the sense of 'to stop disturbing

led

or interfering with', as in '*Leave/let* the dog alone or it will bite you' and '*leave/let* your mother alone—she is not feeling well'. **Leave alone** can also mean 'leave on one's own, cause to be alone', as in 'Her husband went away and left her alone', but **let alone** cannot be used in this sense. **Let alone** can also mean 'not to mention, without considering', as in 'They cannot afford proper food, let alone a holiday', but **leave alone** should not be used in this sense.

led *see* **lead**.

legible and **readable** are not interchangeable. **Legible** means 'able to be deciphered or made out', as in 'His writing is scarcely legible'. **Readable** can also be used in this sense, as in 'His handwriting is just not readable'. However **readable** is also used to mean 'able to be read with interest or enjoyment', as in 'He is an expert on the subject but I think his books are simply not readable' and 'I find her novels very readable but my friend does not like her style'.

legion has three meanings. It refers to 'a unit of the ancient Roman army', as in 'Caesar's legions', and to 'a very large number', as in 'the pop star has legions of admirers'. As an adjective **legion** means 'very many, numerous', as in 'His faults are legion'.

legionnaire is frequently misspelt. Note the double *n*. The word refers to 'a member, or former member, of a military legion, for example, the French Foreign Legion'. In modern usage it is most likely to be found in the phrase **legionnaires' disease**, a kind of pneumonia first discovered in 1976 at a meeting of the American Legion.

leisure is frequently misspelt. Note the *ei* combination. It is pronounced *lezh*-er. In American English it is pronounced *leezh*-er. **Leisure** means 'time spent away from work or duties', as in 'He works a lot of overtime and has very little leisure'. It is frequently used as an adjective, as in 'leisure time' and 'leisure pursuits'.

lend and **loan** can cause confusion. **Lend** is used as a verb in British English to mean 'to allow someone the use of temporarily', as in 'Can you lend me a pen?' and 'His father refused to lend him any money'. **Loan** is a noun meaning 'something lent, the temporary use of', as in 'They thanked her for the loan of her car'. In American English **loan** is used as a verb to mean **lend**, and this use is becoming common in Britain although it is still regarded as not quite acceptable.

length, as in 'measure the length of the room', is frequently misspelt. Note the *g*, which is sometimes wrongly omitted.

lengthways and **lengthwise** are used interchangeably, as in 'fold the tablecloth lengthways/lengthwise' and 'measure the room lengthwise/lengthways'.

lengthy and **long** are not interchangeable. **Lengthy** means 'excessively long', as in 'We had a lengthy wait before we saw the doctor' and 'It was such a lengthy speech that most of the audience got bored'. **Lengthy** is frequently misspelt. Note the *g*.

leopard is frequently misspelt. Note the *o*. It is the name of a wild animal of the cat family, as in 'leopards stalking deer'.

less and **fewer** are often confused. Less means 'a smaller amount or quantity of' and is the comparative form of 'little'. It is found in sentences such as 'less milk', 'less responsibility' and 'less noise'. **Fewer** means 'a smaller number of' and is the comparative of 'few'. It is found in sentences such as 'buy fewer bottles of milk', 'have fewer responsibilities', have fewer opportunities' and 'hear fewer noises'. **Less** is commonly wrongly used where **fewer** is correct. It is common but ungrammatical to say or write 'less bottles of milk' and 'less queues in the shops during the week'.

leukaemia is frequently misspelt. Note the *eu*, *ae* and *ia* combinations. It is pronounced with the emphasis on the second syllable, as loo-*kee*-mia. The word refers to 'a type of cancer in which there is an abnormal increase in the number of white corpuscles', as in 'children suffering from leukaemia'.

liable to and **likely to** both express probability. They mean much the same except that **liable to** suggests that the probability is based on past experience or habit. 'He is liable to lose his temper' suggests that he has been in the habit of doing so in the past. 'He is likely to lose his temper' suggests that he will probably lose his temper, given the situation, but that the probability is not based on how he has reacted in the past. This distinction is not always adhered to, and some people use the terms interchangeably.

liaison, meaning 'communication and cooperation', as in 'Liaison between departments is essential', is frequently misspelt. Note the *i* before the *s*. This is often omitted in error. Note also the *i* before the *s* in **liaise**, which means 'to act as a link or go-between', as in 'You must liaise with your colleague in the other department'.

libel and **slander** both refer to defamatory statements against someone but they are not interchangeable. **Libel** refers to defamation that is written down, printed or drawn, as in 'The politician sued the newspaper for libel when it falsely accused him of fraud'. **Slander** refers to defamation in spoken form, as in 'She heard that one of her neighbours was spreading slander about her'. Both **libel** and **slander** can act as verbs, as in 'bring a suit against the newspaper for libelling him' and 'think that one of her neighbours was slandering her'. Note that the verb **libel** doubles the *l* in the past participle, past tense and present participle, as **libelled** and **libelling**.

library, meaning a collection of books or the place where it is kept, should be pronounced *lib*-ra-ri although it is quite often pronounced *lib*-ri.

licence and **license** are liable to cause confusion in British English. **Licence** is a noun meaning 'an official document showing that permission has been given to do, use or own something', as in 'require a licence to have a stall in the market', 'have a licence to drive a car', and 'apply for a pilot's licence'. **License** is a verb meaning 'to provide someone with a licence', as in 'The council have licensed him as a street trader', 'The restaurant has been licensed to sell alcohol'. Note **licensed grocer** and **licensing laws** but **off-licence**. In American English both the noun and verb are spelt **license**.

lie *see* **lay**.

lieu *see* **in lieu**.

lieutenant

lieutenant is often misspelt. Note the *ieu* combination. In British English the word is pronounced lef-*ten*-ant. The word originally referred to an army or naval rank but is also used to mean 'a deputy, a chief assistant', as in 'The owner of the factory was unavailable but we talked to some of his lieutenants'.

lifelong and **livelong** are liable to be confused. **Lifelong** means 'lasting a lifetime', as in 'He never realized his lifelong ambition of going to Australia' and 'her lifelong membership of the society'. **Livelong** is found in rather literary contexts and means 'whole, entire', as in 'The children played on the beach the livelong day'. In **livelong** the first syllable is pronounced like 'live', as in 'live a long time'.

lighted and **lit** can both be used as the past participle and past tense of the verb 'to light'. **Lit** is the more common form, as in 'We lit the fire early' and 'They lit the birthday candles'. **Lighted** is used when the past participle is used as an adjective, as in 'children playing with lighted matches' and 'The fire was started by a lighted match being thrown away'.

lightning and **lightening** are liable to be confused because they sound alike. **Lightning** refers to 'flashes of light produced by atmospheric electricity', as in 'The child was afraid of thunder and lightning' and 'He was hit by lightning and was killed'. **Lightning** is also used as an adjective meaning 'happening very quickly, suddenly or briefly', as in 'The police made a lightning strike on the nightclub', 'She made a lightning decision to go on holiday', and 'The visitors made a lightning tour of the factory'. **Lightening** is the present participle of the verb 'to lighten', as in 'lightening her hair with peroxide' and 'Lightening his work load is a priority'.

light years are a measure of distance, not time. A **light year** is the distance travelled by light in one year (about six million, million miles) and is a term used in astronomy. **Light years** are often referred to in an informal context when time, not distance, is involved, as in 'Owning their own house seemed light years away' and 'It seems light years since we had a holiday'.

likable *see* **likeable**.

like tends to cause confusion. It is a preposition meaning 'resembling, similar to', as in 'houses like castles', 'gardens like jungles', 'actors like Olivier', 'She looks like her mother', 'She plays like an expert', 'The child swims like a fish' and 'Like you, he cannot stand cruelty to animals'. To be grammatically correct **like** should not be used as a conjunction. Thus 'The house looks like it has been deserted' is incorrect. It should read 'The house looks as though/if it has been deserted'. Similarly, 'Like his mother said, he has had to go to hospital' should read 'As his mother said, he has had to go to hospital'.

likeable and **likable** are both acceptable spellings. The word means 'pleasant, agreeable, friendly', as in 'He is a likeable/likable young man'.

likely to *see* **liable to**.

lineage and **linage** do not mean the same thing. **Lineage** refers to 'line of descent, ancestry', as in 'a family of noble lineage'. **Linage** is rather a specialist term meaning 'number of written or printed lines', as in 'The free-

liqueur

lance journalist was paid on a linage basis'. **Linage** can also be spelt **lineage**.

liqueur and **liquor** are liable to be confused. **Liqueur** refers to 'a sweet alcoholic drink taken after dinner', as in 'have a liqueur with one's coffee'. **Liquor** refers to 'any strong alcoholic drink', as in 'prefer soft drinks to liquor'.

liquidate and **liquidize** are liable to be confused. **Liquidate** is frequently used in a financial context. It means 'to settle or pay', as in 'to liquidate a debt'; 'to terminate the operations of a firm by assessment of debts and use the assets towards paying off the debts', as in 'forced to liquidate the firm'; 'to convert into cash', as in 'liquidate one's assets'. In an informal context **liquidate** means 'to kill', as in 'paid to liquidate a member of the enemy gang'. **Liquidize** means 'to make liquid, especially to pulverize into a pulp', as in 'liquidize the vegetables to make a soup'.

liquor *see* **liqueur**.

lit *see* **lighted**.

literal, literary and **literate** are liable to be confused. **Literal** means 'word for word, exact', as in 'a literal translation', 'a literal interpretation of the words'. **Literary** means 'referring to literature', as in 'come from a literary background', 'have literary interests' and 'literary criticism'. **Literate** means 'able to read and write', as in 'children who are leaving school scarcely literate', and 'well-educated', as in 'a very literate family'.

literally is frequently used simply to add emphasis to an idea rather than to indicate that the word, phrase, etc, used is to be interpreted word for word. Thus, 'She was literally tearing her hair out' does not mean that she was pulling her hair out by the handful but that she was very angry, anxious, frustrated, etc.

literary *see* **literal**.

livelong *see* **lifelong**.

livid and **lurid** are liable to be confused although they mean different things. **Livid** means 'discoloured, of a greyish tinge', as in 'a livid bruise on her face', and 'furious', as in 'When he saw his damaged car he was livid'. **Lurid** means 'sensational, shocking', as in 'give the lurid details about finding the body', and 'garish, glaringly bright', as in 'wear a lurid shade of green'.

living room *see* **sitting room**.

loan *see* **lend**.

loath, loathe and **loth** are not all interchangeable. **Loath** and **loth** mean 'reluctant, unwilling', as in 'We were loath/loth to punish the children' and 'They are loath/loth to move house again'. **Loathe** means 'to hate very much, to detest', as in 'She loathes dishonesty' and 'The rivals loathe each other'. The *th* in **loath** and **loth** is pronounced as the *th* in 'bath', but the *th* in **loathe** is pronounced like the *th* in 'bathe'.

longevity, meaning 'long life', is liable to be mispronounced. It should be pronounced lon-*jev*-iti. Some people pronounce it lon-*gev*-iti, but this is rarer.

loo *see* **toilet**.

loose, loosen and **lose** are liable to be confused. **Loose** and **loosen** are related but not **lose**. **Loose** is an adjective meaning 'not tight', as in 'His clothes are loose now

159

lose

that he has lost weight', and 'free, not confined', as in
'The cows are loose'. It is also a verb meaning 'to undo',
as in 'loose the knot', or 'set free', as in 'loose the pack
of hounds'. **Loosen** means 'to make less tight', as in
'He has put on weight and so he has had to loosen his
belt'. **Lose** is a verb meaning 'not to be able to find, to
mislay', as in 'I always lose one glove' and 'They may
lose their way'. **Loose** is pronounced loos, but **lose** is
pronounced looz.

lose *see* **loose**.

lots of and **a lot of**, meaning 'many' and 'much', should
be used only in informal contexts', as in '"I've got lots
of toys," said the child' and 'You're talking a lot of rubbish'. They should be avoided in formal prose.

loth *see* **loath**.

lounge *see* **sitting room**.

low and **lowly** are not interchangeable. **Low** means 'not
high', as in 'a low fence', 'a low level of income', 'speak
in a low voice' and 'her low status in the firm'. It can
also mean 'despicable, contemptible', as in 'That was a
low trick' or 'He's a low creature'. **Lowly** means 'hum-
ble', as in 'of lowly birth' and 'the peasant's lowly
abode'.

lowly *see* **low**.

lunch and **luncheon** both refer to a meal eaten in the middle of the day. **Lunch**, as in 'a business lunch' and 'have
just a snack for lunch', is by far the more usual term.
Luncheon, as in 'give a luncheon party for the visiting
celebrity', is a very formal word and is becoming increasingly uncommon. *See also* **dinner**.

lurid *see* **livid**.

luxuriant, luxurious and **luxury** are liable to be confused. They have completely different meanings. **Luxuriant** means 'profuse, growing thickly and strongly', as in 'the luxuriant vegetation of the area' and 'her luxuriant hair'. **Luxurious** means 'referring to or characterized by luxury', as in 'a luxurious lifestyle' and 'live in luxurious surroundings'. **Luxury** is a noun meaning 'great ease or comfort based on wealth', as in 'live in luxury' and 'a hotel providing luxury'. It also means 'something that is enjoyable but is not essential and is usually expensive', as in 'no money for luxuries' and 'spend money on luxuries such as champagne'. **Luxury** can be used as an adjective, as in 'a luxury hotel' and 'a shop selling luxury goods'.

M

macabre, meaning 'connected with death' or 'gruesome', as in 'a macabre tale about attacks on people in the graveyard' and 'policemen sickened by a particularly macabre murder', is liable to be misspelt. Note the *re* ending.

machinations, meaning 'devious plots or schemes', as in 'They were plotting to kill the king but their machinations were discovered', should be pronounced mak-in-*ay*-shunz but mash-in *ay*-shunz is becoming increasingly common in modern usage.

madam and **madame** are liable to be confused. **Madam** is the English-language form of the French **madame**. It is a form of formal of address for a woman, as in 'Please come this way, madam'. It is used in formal letters when the name of the woman being written to is not known, as in 'Dear Madam'. **Madam** can be written either with a capital letter or a lower-case letter. **Madam** is pronounced *mad*-am, with the emphasis on the first syllable. **Madame**, which is the French equivalent of 'Mrs', is occasionally found in English, as in Madame Tussaud's, and is pronounced in the same way as **madam**. In French **madame** is pronounced ma-*dam*.

majority and **minority** are opposites. **Majority** means

162

'more than half the total number of', as in 'The majority of the pupils live locally' and 'the younger candidate received the majority of the votes'. **Minority** means less than half the total number of', as in 'A small minority of the football fans caused trouble' and 'Only a minority of the committee voted against the motion'. **Majority** and **minority** should not be used to describe the greater or lesser part of a single thing. Thus it is wrong to say 'The majority of the book is uninteresting'.

male, masculine and **mannish** all refer to the sex that is not female but the words are used in different ways. **Male** is the opposite of 'female' and refers to the sex of a person or animal, as in 'no male person may enter', 'a male nurse', 'a male elephant' and 'the male reproductive system'. **Masculine** is the opposite of 'feminine' and refers to people or their characteristics. It refers to characteristics, etc, that are traditionally considered to be typically **male**. Examples of its use include 'a very masculine young man', 'a deep, masculine voice'. It can be used of women, as in 'She has a masculine walk' and 'She wears masculine clothes'. When used of women it is often derogatory and is sometimes replaced with **mannish**, which is derogatory, as in 'women with mannish haircuts'. **Male** can also be used as a noun, as in 'the male of the species' 'of the robins, the male is more colourful' and 'the title can be held only by males'.

man causes a great deal of controversy. To avoid being sexist it should be avoided when it really means 'person'. 'We must find the right man for the job' should read 'We must find the right person for the job'. Similarly, 'All men have a right to a reasonable standard of living' should read 'All people have a right to a reasonable standard of living' or 'Everyone has a right to a reasonable standard of living'. Problems also arise with compounds, such as 'chairman'. In such situations 'person' is often used, as in 'chairperson'. Man is also used to mean 'mankind, humankind', as in 'Man is mortal' and 'Man has the power of thought'. Some people also object to this usage and consider it sexist. They advocate using 'humankind' or 'the human race'.

manageable is liable to be misspelt. Note the *e* before the ending *-able*. It means 'able to be controlled, easily controlled', as in 'a task of scarcely manageable proportions' and 'The nanny will not take the job unless the children are manageable'.

mandatory is liable to be mispronounced. The emphasis should be on the first syllable, as *man*-da-tor-i. It means 'required by law, compulsory', as in 'A visa is mandatory for some countries' and 'He was fined for not making the mandatory payment'.

manoeuvre is frequently misspelt. Note the *oeu* combination and the *-re* ending. In American English the *o* is omitted and the ending is *er*. It means 'a movement or action, especially one requiring skill and dexterity', as in 'We were admiring the manoeuvres of the skaters', and 'a skilful, and often complicated and deceptive plan', as in 'his manoeuvres to discredit his boss and obtain his job'. **Manoeuvre** is also a verb meaning 'to move or position, especially with skill or dexterity', as in 'racing drivers manoeuvring their cars on a muddy circuit', and 'to guide or manipulate skilfully and usually cunningly', as in 'She manoeuvred herself into a position of trust'.

mantel and **mantle** are liable to be confused. **Mantel** is more usually called **mantelpiece** and refers to 'a shelf above a fireplace', as in 'a vase of flowers on the mantelpiece'. **Mantelpiece** is frequently misspelt as 'mantlepiece'. **Mantle** is an old word for a cloak and is now found mostly in the sense of 'covering', as in 'a mantle of autumn leaves on the grass'.

many is used in more formal contexts rather than 'a lot of' or 'lots of', as in 'The judge said the accused had had many previous convictions'. **Many** is often used in the negative in both formal and informal contexts, as in 'They don't have many friends' and 'She won't find many apples on the trees now'.

margarine causes confusion with reference to pronunciation. Formerly the usual pronunciation was mar-ga-reen but now the most common pronunciation is mar-ja-reen. It refers to 'a substitute for butter'.

masculine *see* **male**.

masterful and **masterly** are liable to be confused although they mean different things. **Masterful** means 'able to control others, dominating', as in 'She likes masterful men' and 'The country needs a masterful ruler'. **Masterly** means 'very skilful', as in 'admire his masterly handling of the situation' and 'their masterly defeat of the opposing team'.

mattress is often misspelt. Note the double *t* and double *s*. The word means 'a fabric case filled with soft or

may

springy material used for sleeping on', as in 'He likes to sleep on a firm mattress'.

may *see* **can**.

maybe and **may be** are liable to be confused although they have different meanings. **Maybe** means 'perhaps', as in 'Maybe they lost their way' and 'He said, "Maybe" when I asked him if he was going'. It is used in more informal contexts than 'perhaps'. **May be** is used in such sentences as 'He may be poor but he is very generous' and 'They may be a little late'.

mayoress means 'the wife or partner of a male mayor', as in 'an official dinner for the mayor and mayoress'. A mayor who is a woman is called either 'mayor' or 'lady mayor'.

meaningful originally meant 'full of meaning', as in 'make very few meaningful statements' and 'There was a meaningful silence'. In modern usage it has come to mean 'important, significant, serious', as in 'not interested in a meaningful relationship' and 'seeking a meaningful career'. The word now tends to be very much over-used.

means in the sense of 'way, method' can be either a singular or plural noun, as in 'The means of defeating them is in our hands' and 'Many different means of financing the project have been investigated'. **Means** in the sense of 'wealth' and 'resources' is plural, as in 'His means are not sufficient to support two families'.

media gives rise to confusion. In the form of **the media** it is commonly applied to the press, to newspapers, television and radio, as in 'The politician claimed that he was being harassed by the media'. **Media** is a plural form of 'medium', meaning 'means of communication', as in 'television is a powerful medium'. In modern usage **media** is beginning to be used as a singular noun, as in 'The politician blamed a hostile media for his misfortunes', but this is still regarded as being an incorrect use.

mediaeval and **medieval** are both acceptable spellings. **Mediaeval** was formerly the only acceptable spelling in British English and **medieval** was considered the American spelling. However, in modern usage **medieval** is the more common term in British English. The word means 'relating to the Middle Ages', as in 'medieval knights' and 'medieval castles'.

mediocre is liable to be misspelt. Note the -*re* ending It is a common error to make this -*er*. It means 'not very good, of indifferent quality', as in 'a mediocre pupil unlikely to do well in the exam' and 'His work is at best mediocre'. It is pronounced meed-i-*ok*-er, with the emphasis on the third syllable.

melted and **molten** are not interchangeable although they are both formed the verb 'to melt'. **Melted** is the past participle and the past tense of 'melt', as in 'The ice cream had melted all over the child's clothes' and 'The chocolate melted in the heat'. **Molten** means 'melted or made liquid by heating to very high temperature', as in 'molten rock' and 'molten lava'.

memento is liable to be misspelt. Note the *e* following the first *m*. It is a common error to put *o* instead. The plural form is either **mementos** or **mementoes**. **Memento** refers to 'something kept as a reminder', as in 'He bought her a scarf as a memento of their trip to Paris'.

metal

metal and **mettle** are liable to be confused because they sound alike. **Metal** refers to 'a member of a group of mineral substances that are opaque and good conductors of heat and electricity', as in 'appliances made of metal' and 'cutlery made of plastic, not metal'. **Mettle** means 'endurance, courage, strength of character', as in 'show his mettle by learning to walk again' and 'give the candidates a chance to prove their mettle'.

metaphor is a figure of speech in which a word or phrase is used to suggest a similarity to something else. The similarity is not introduced by 'like' or 'as' as it is in the case of a 'simile'. Examples include 'She was a rose among thorns' and 'Their new product is the jewel in the firm's crown', 'He is a pillar of the community' and 'His mother is a clinging vine'.

meter *see* **metre**.

mettle *see* **metal**.

middle *see* **centre**.

migraine causes problems with regard to pronunciation. It is pronounced *mee*-grayn in British English but the American pronunciation of *mi*-grayn, in which the first syllable rhymes with 'eye', is sometimes used in Britain. **Migraine** refers to 'a severe and recurrent type of headache, often accompanied by vomiting', as in 'She had to lie down in a darkened room because of her migraine'.

mileage and **milage** are both acceptable spellings for 'the distance travelled or measured in miles', as in 'The car is a bargain, given the low mileage'. However **mileage** is much more common than **milage**. The word also means

168

informally 'benefit, advantage', as in 'The politician got a lot of mileage from the scandal surrounding his opponent' and 'There's not much mileage in pursuing that particular line of inquiry'.

militate and **mitigate** are liable to be confused. **Militate** means 'to have or serve as a strong influence against', as in 'Their lack of facts militated against the success of their application' and 'His previous record will militate against his chances of going free'. **Mitigate** means 'to alleviate', as in 'try to mitigate the suffering of the refugees', or 'moderate', as in 'mitigate the severity of the punishment'.

millennium is liable to be misspelt. Note the double *n* which is frequently omitted in error. The plural form is **millennia**. **Millennium** refers to 'a period of 1000 years', as in 'rock changes taking place over several millennia'. In religious terms it refers to 'the thousand-year reign of Christ prophesied in the Bible'.

millionaire is liable to be misspelt. Note the single *n*. It means 'a person who has a million pounds or dollars' or 'a very wealthy person', as in 'millionaires who spend all their time travelling around the world'.

mimic is liable to be misspelt in its past participle, past tense and present tense. These are respectively **mimicked** and **mimicking**. Note the *k* in these forms. The word means 'to imitate', as in 'The pupil was mimicking the teacher when she walked into the room'. Note that the noun **mimicry** does not have a *k*.

miniature is frequently misspelt. Note the *i* after the *n*. This is often omitted in error. It means 'very small in

minority

size', as in 'beautiful miniature coffee cups' and 'a miniature bottle of whisky'. It can also be a noun meaning 'a very small copy or model', as in 'a miniature of the Tower of London', or 'a very small detailed painting, as in 'admire the miniatures in the art gallery'.

minority *see* **majority**.

minuscule is liable to be misspelt. Note the *u* before the *s*. It is a common error to put an *i*. The word is pronounced *min*-iskyool. It means 'extremely small, tiny', as in 'only a minuscule amount of coffee left'.

miscellaneous is very frequently misspelt. Note the *c* after the *s*, the double *l* and the *-eous* ending. The word means 'of various kinds', as in 'a miscellaneous collection of articles for the jumble sale' and 'Some money will have to be allocated for miscellaneous expense'.

mischievous is frequently misspelt and mispronounced. Note the *ie* combination and the absence of *i* before *ous*. It is pronounced *mis*-chiv-is, not mis-*cheev*-is.

Miss *see* **Ms**.

misspelled and **misspelt** are often wrongly spelt. Note the double *s*. Both **misspelled** and **misspelt** are acceptable spellings of the past tense and past participle of the verb 'to misspell'. **Misspell** means 'to spell wrongly'.

misuse *see* **abuse**.

mitigate *see* **militate**.

mnemonic refers to 'something that aids the memory'. For example, some people use a **mnemonic** in the form of a verse to remind them how to spell a word or to recall a date. The word is liable to be misspelt and mispronounced. Note the initial *m*, which is silent. **Mnemonic**

is pronounced nim-*on*-ik, with the emphasis on the second syllable.

moccasin is frequently misspelt. Note the double *c* and single *s*. The word refers to 'a flat-soled shoe made of soft leather', as in 'She was wearing moccasins and so he did not hear her approach'.

modern and **modernistic** are not quite the same. **Modern** means 'referring to the present time or recent times', as in 'the politics of modern times' and 'a production of Shakespeare's *Twelfth Night* in modern dress'. It also means 'using the newest techniques, equipment, buildings, etc, as in 'a modern shopping centre' and 'a modern office complex'. **Modernistic** means 'characteristic of modern ideas, fashions, etc, and is often used in a derogatory way, as in 'She says she hates that modernistic furniture'.

modus vivendi refers to 'a practical, sometimes temporary, arrangement or compromise by which people who are in conflict can live or work together', as in 'The two opposing parties on the committee will have to reach a modus vivendi if any progress is to be made'. It is a Latin phrase that literally means 'a way of living' and is pronounced *mo*-dus viv-*en*-di.

molten *see* **melted**.

momentary and **momentous** are liable to be confused. They look rather similar but they are completely different in meaning. **Momentary** means 'lasting for a very short time', as in 'There was a momentary pause' and 'enjoy a momentary success'. It is derived from the noun 'moment' in the sense of 'a very brief period of time'.

moral

Momentous means 'very important, of great significance', as in 'a momentous incident that led to war'. It is derived from the noun 'moment' in the sense of 'importance, significance', as in 'a meeting of moment'. In **momentary** the emphasis is on the first syllable, as *mom*-en-tar-i or *mom*-en-tri. In **momentous** the stress is on the second syllable, as mom-*en*-tus.

moral and **morale** are liable to be confused although they are different in meaning. **Moral** means 'concerning the principles of right and wrong', as in 'the decline of moral standards' and 'criticize his actions on moral grounds'. **Morale** means 'state of confidence, enthusiasm, etc', as in 'It was a blow to his morale when he failed to get the job' and 'The morale of the country was very low during the recession'. **Moral** is pronounced with the emphasis on the first syllable, as in *mor*-al. **Morale** is pronounced with the emphasis on the second syllable'.

more is used to form the comparative of adjectives and adverbs that do not form the comparative by adding *-er*. This usually applies to longer adjectives, as in 'more beautiful', 'more gracious', 'more useful', and 'more flattering'. **More** should not be used with adjectives that have a comparative ending already. Thus it is wrong to write 'more happier'. **Most** is used in the same way to form the superlative of adjectives and adverbs, as in 'most beautiful', 'most gracious' etc.

Moslem *see* **Muslim**.

most *see* **more**.

motif and **motive** are liable to be confused although they have entirely different meanings. **Motif** refers to 'a theme

172

or idea that is repeated and developed in a work of music or literature', as in 'a motif of suicide runs through the whole novel'. It also means 'a decorative design or pattern', as in 'curtains with a flower motif'. **Motive** refers to 'the reason for a course of action', as in 'There appears to have been no motive for the murder' and 'What was her motive in telling lies about him?' **Motif** is pronounced with the emphasis on the second syllable, as mo-*teef*. **Motive** is pronounced with the emphasis on the first syllable, as *mo*-tiv.

motive *see* **motif.**

movable and **moveable** are both possible spellings but **movable** is the more common, as in 'movable possessions' and 'machines with movable parts'.

Ms, Mrs and **Miss** are all used before the names of women in addressing them and in letter-writing. Formerly **Mrs** was used before the name of a married woman and **Miss** before the name of an unmarried woman or girl. In modern usage **Ms** is often used instead of **Miss** or **Mrs**. This is sometimes because the marital status of the woman is not known and sometimes from a personal preference. Many people feel that since no distinction is made between married and unmarried men when they are being addressed, no distinction should be made between married and unmarried women. On the other hand some people, particularly older women, object to the use of **Ms**.

much, except in negative sentences, is used mainly in rather formal contexts, as in 'They own much property'. 'A great deal of' is often used instead, as in 'They own a great deal of property'. In informal contexts 'a lot of' is often used instead of **much**, as in 'a lot of rubbish' not 'much rubbish'. **Much** is used in negative sentences, as in 'They do not have much money'.

Muslim and **Moslem** refer to to 'a follower of the Islamic faith'. In modern usage **Muslim** is the preferred term rather than the older spelling **Moslem**.

N

naïve causes problems with reference to both spelling and pronunciation. It can be spelt either **naïve** or **naive** and is pronounced ni-*eev*, with the emphasis on the second syllable, and the first syllable rhyming with 'my'. The accent on the *ï* (called a diaeresis) indicates that the two vowels *a* and *i* are to be pronounced separately. **Naive** means either 'innocent' or 'too ready to believe what one is told', as in 'You would have to be incredibly naive to believe his excuses'.

naturalist and **naturist** are liable to be confused. They look rather similar but have completely different meanings. **Naturalist** refers to 'a person who studies animals, birds and plants', as in 'naturalists collecting some of the local wild flowers'. **Naturist** refers to 'a person who practises naturism or nudism', as in 'naturists with their own secluded beaches'. **Naturist** can also be an adjective, as in 'naturist beaches'.

naught and **nought** are not totally interchangeable. **Naught** means 'nothing', as in 'All his projects came to naught', and is rather a formal or literary word in this sense. **Naught** is also a less usual spelling of **nought**, which means 'zero' when it is regarded as a number, as in 'nought point one (0.1)'.

naval

naval and **navel** are liable to be confused. They sound alike but they have entirely different meanings. **Naval** means 'referring to the navy', as in 'a naval base' and 'naval personnel'. **Navel** refers to 'a small hollow in the middle of the abdomen where the umbilical cord was attached at birth', as in 'The baby has an infection in the navel'.

nearby and **near by** can cause problems. **Nearby** can be either an adjective, as in 'the nearby village', or an adverb, as in 'Her mother lives nearby'. **Near by** is an adverb, as in 'He doesn't have far to go—he lives near by'. In other words, the adverbial sense can be spelt either **nearby** or **near by**.

necessarily is traditionally pronounced with the emphasis on the first syllable, but this is often very difficult to say except when one is speaking exceptionally carefully. Because of this difficulty it is often pronounced with the emphasis on the third syllable although it is considered by many people to be incorrect.

necessary is frequently misspelt. Note the single *c* and double *s*. It means 'that cannot be done without', as in 'make only necessary purchases' and 'It may be necessary to take him to hospital'.

née is used to indicate the maiden or family name of a married woman, as in 'Jane Jones, née Smith'. It is derived from French, being the feminine form of the French word for 'born'. It can be spelt either with an acute accent or not—**née** or **nee**.

negligent and **negligible** are liable to be confused. **Negligent** means 'not giving proper attention, careless', as in

176

'mothers accused of being negligent by not making sure their children attend school' and 'He said that his wife had died because of a negligent doctor'. **Negligible** means 'extremely small', as in 'a negligible difference between the prices' and 'lose a negligible amount of weight'. Note the *-ible* ending in **negligible**.

neither as an adjective or a pronoun takes a singular verb, as in 'Neither parent will come' and 'Neither of them wishes to come'. In the **neither ... nor** construction, a singular verb is used if both parts of the construction are singular, as in 'Neither Jane nor Mary was present'. If both parts are plural the verb is plural, as in 'Neither their parents nor their grandparents are willing to look after them'. If the construction involves a mixture of singular and plural, the verb traditionally agrees with the subject that is nearest it, as in 'Neither her mother nor her grandparents are going to come' and 'Neither her grandparents nor her mother is going to come'. If pronouns are used, the nearer one governs the verb as in 'Neither they nor he is at fault' and 'Neither he nor they are at fault'.

never in the sense of 'did not', as in 'He never saw the other car before he hit it', should be used in only very informal contexts. **Never** means 'at no time, on no occasion', as in 'He will never agree to their demands' and 'She has never been poor'. It is also used as a negative for the sake of emphasis, as in 'He never so much as smiled'.

nevertheless and **none the less** mean the same thing, as in 'He has very little money. Nevertheless/none the less he gives generously to charity'. **None the less** is usually written as three words but **nevertheless** is spelt as one word. In modern usage **none the less** is sometimes written as one word, as **nonetheless**.

next and **this** can cause confusion. **Next** in one of its senses is used to mean the day of the week, month of the year, season of the year, etc, that will follow next, as in 'They are coming next Tuesday', 'We are going on holiday next June' and 'They to be married next summer'. **This** can also be used in this sense and so ambiguity can occur. Some people use **this** to refer to the very next Tuesday, June, summer, etc, and use **next** for the one after that. Thus someone might say on Sunday, 'I'll see you next Friday', meaning the first Friday to come, but someone else might take that to mean a week on from that because they would refer to the first Friday to come as 'this Friday'. The only solution is to make sure exactly which day, week, season, etc, the other person is referring to.

nice originally meant 'fine, subtle, requiring precision', as in 'There is rather a nice distinction between the two words', but it is widely used in the sense of 'pleasant, agreeable, etc', as in 'She is a nice person' and 'We had a nice time at the picnic'. It is overused and alternative adjectives should be found to avoid this, as in 'She is an amiable person' and 'We had an enjoyable time at the picnic'.

niceness and **nicety** are both nouns formed from 'nice' but they do not mean the same thing. **Niceness** is the noun from 'nice' in the sense of 'pleasant, agreeable', as in 'They appreciated the niceness of the old lady' and 'The niceness of the climate is the best part of the holiday resort'. **Nicety** is the noun from 'nice' in the sense of 'fine, subtle', as in 'the nicety of the distinction between the two words'.

niche causes problems with reference to both pronunciation and spelling'. The most common pronunciation is *nitch*, but *neech*, following the French pronunciation, is also a possibility. Note the absence of *t* in the spelling.

nimby *see* **acronym**.

nobody *see* **no one**.

none can be used with either a singular verb or plural verb. Examples of sentences using a singular verb include 'There is none of the food left' and 'None of the work is good enough' and 'None of the coal is to be used today'. In sentences where none is used with a plural noun the verb was traditionally still singular, as in 'None of the books is suitable' and 'None of the parcels is undamaged'. This is still the case in formal contexts but, in the case of informal contexts, a plural verb is often used in modern usage, as in 'None of these things are any good'.

none the less *see* **nevertheless**.

no one and **no-one** are interchangeable but the word is never written 'noone', unlike 'everyone'. **No one** and **no-one** are used with a singular verb, as in 'No one is allowed to leave' and 'No one is anxious to leave'. They are used by some people with a plural personal pronoun or possessive case when attempts are being made to avoid sexism, as in 'No one is expected to take their child away', although the singular form is grammatically correct, as in 'No one is expected to take his/her child away'. 'No one is expected to take his child away' is sexist. Nobody is interchangeable with no one, as in 'You must tell no one/nobody about this'.

nor is used as part of the **neither ... nor** construction, and this is dealt with under **neither**. It is also used in such constructions as 'He plays neither golf nor tennis' and 'We were given neither food nor drink' and 'He does not watch television. Nor does he go to the cinema'. In some contexts **nor** is interchangeable with **or**, as in 'The shop is not open on Saturday nor/or Sunday' and 'They have no food nor/or drink'. **Nor** can be used at the start of a sentence, as in 'He does not believe her. Nor does he trust her'.

notable *see* **noticeable**.

noticeable and **notable** are liable to be confused. They are both related to 'note' but they mean different things. **Noticeable** means 'obvious', as in 'She had a noticeable bruise on her cheek' and 'The hostile atmosphere between them was noticeable to everyone'. **Notable** means 'of note, remarkable', as in 'his notable achievements in the world of business' and 'one of the most notable poets of the century'.

not only is frequently used in a construction with 'but also', as in 'We have not only the best candidate but also the most efficient organization' and 'The organizers of the fete not only made a great deal of money for charity but also gave a great many people a great deal of pleasure'.

nought *see* **naught**.

noxious and **obnoxious** are liable to be confused. They both refer to unpleasantness or harmfulness but they are used in different contexts. **Noxious** is used of a substance, fumes, etc, and means 'harmful, poisonous', as in 'firemen overcome by noxious fumes' and 'delinquent children having a noxious influence on the rest of the class'. **Obnoxious** means 'unpleasant, nasty, offensive', as in 'He has the most obnoxious neighbours' and 'The child's parents let him off with the most obnoxious behaviour'. **Noxious** is used in formal and technical contexts rather than **obnoxious**.

nubile originally meant 'old enough to marry, marriageable' as in 'he has five nubile daughters'. In modern usage **nubile** is frequently used in the sense of 'sexually attractive', as in 'admiring the nubile girls sunbathing on the beach' and 'nubile models posing for magazine illustrations'.

numbers can be written in either figures or words. It is largely a matter of taste which method is adopted. As long as the method is consistent it does not really matter. Some establishments, such as a publishing house or a newspaper office, will have a house style. For example, some of them prefer to have numbers up to 10 written in words, as in 'They have two boys and three girls'. If this system is adopted, guidance should be sought as to whether a mixture of figures and words in the same sentence is acceptable, as in 'We have 12 cups but only six saucers', or whether the rule should be broken in such situations as 'We have twelve cups but only six saucers'.

nutritional

nutritional and **nutricious** are liable to be confused. They both refer to 'nutrition, the process of giving and receiving nourishment' but mean different things. **Nutritional** means 'referring to nutrition', as in 'doubts about the nutritional value of some fast foods' and 'people who do not receive the minimum nutritional requirements'. **Nutritious** means 'nourishing, of high value as a food', as in 'nourishing homemade soups' and 'something slightly more nourishing than a plate of chips'.

O

O and **Oh** are both forms of an exclamation made at the beginning of a sentence. **Oh** is the usual spelling, as in 'Oh well. It's Friday tomorrow' and 'Oh dear, the baby's crying again'. **O** is considerably rarer and is used in literary contexts in poetry, hymns etc, as in 'O come all ye faithful'. Both **Oh** and **O** are always spelt with an initial capital letter.

object refers to the noun, pronoun or phrase that is affected by the action of the verb. In the sentence 'He eventually married the girl', 'girl' is the object. In the sentence 'They beat him up badly', 'him' is the object. In the sentence 'She received a bunch of flowers', 'bunch of flowers' is the object. An object may be *direct* or *indirect*. The examples shown above are all *direct objects*. In the sentence 'She gave the child a book', 'book' is the *direct object* and 'the child' is the *indirect object*. In the sentence 'I bought him an apple', 'him' is the *indirect object*. In the case of *indirect objects*, it is usually possible to rephrase the sentences in which they appear, putting 'to' or 'for' before the *indirect object*, as in 'She gave a book to the child' and 'I bought an apple for him'. *See* **subject**.

Object can also mean 'aim, goal'—*see* **objective** and **subjective**.

183

objective

   Object is also a verb meaning 'to say that one is not in favour of something, to protest', as in 'They objected to the fact that the decision was taken in their absence'. In the verb sense, **object** is pronounced with the emphasis on the second syllable, as ob-*ject*.

objective and **subjective** are opposites. **Objective** means 'not influenced by personal feelings, attitudes, or prejudices', as in 'She is related to the person accused and so she cannot give an objective view of the situation' and 'It is important that all members of a jury are completely objective'. **Subjective** means 'influenced by personal feelings, attitudes and prejudices', as in 'It is only natural to be subjective in situations regarding one's children' and 'She wrote a very subjective report on the conference and did not stick to the facts'. **Objective** can also be a noun in the sense of 'aim, goal', as in 'Our objective was to make as much money as possible'. **Object** can also be used in this sense, as in 'Their main object is to have a good time'.

oblivious means 'unaware of, unconscious of, not noticing'. Traditionally it is followed by the preposition 'of', as in 'The lovers were oblivious of the rain' and 'When he is reading he is completely oblivious of his surroundings'. In modern usage its use with the preposition 'to' is also considered acceptable, as in 'They were oblivious to the fact that he was cheating them' and 'sleep soundly, oblivious to the noise'.

obnoxious *see* **noxious**.

obscene and **pornographic** are not interchangeable. **Obscene** means 'indecent, especially in a sexual way, offending against the accepted standards of decency', as in 'obscene drawings on the walls of the public toilet' and 'When his car was damaged he let out a stream of obscene language'. **Pornographic** means 'intended to arouse sexual excitement', as in 'pornographic videos' and 'magazines with women shown in pornographic poses'. **Obscene** is frequently misspelt. Note the *c* after the *s*.

observance and **observation** are liable to be confused. They are both derived from the verb 'to observe' but from different senses of it. **Observance** is derived from 'observe' in the sense of 'obey, comply with', as in 'the observance of school rules' and 'the observance of local customs'. It also refers to 'a ritual act or practice', as in 'religious observances'. **Observation** is derived from the verb 'to observe' meaning 'to see, to notice', as in 'keep the patient under observation' and 'From his observation of them they appeared to be acting strangely'. **Observation** also means 'a remark', as in 'The inspector made a few critical observations about the state of the restaurant's kitchens'.

occasion is frequently misspelt. Note the double *c* and single *s*. It is a common error to put a single *c* and double *s*. **Occasion** is a noun meaning 'a particular time', as in 'happen on more than one occasion', and 'a special event or celebration', as in 'the dinner was a formal occasion'. More rarely **occasion** can be used as a verb but it should be restricted to rather formal situations. It means 'to cause, to bring about', as in 'His remarks occasioned a family feud'.

occurrence is very frequently misspelt. Note the double *c*, double *r* and *-ence* ending. It comes from the verb **occur**, 'to happen'. Note also **occurred** and **occurring**. **Occurrence** means 'an event, incident, happening', as in 'Robbery is an everyday occurrence there' and 'The occurrence of tuberculosis is on the increase'.

oculist *see* **optician**.

of is sometimes wrongly used instead of the verb 'to have', as in 'He must of known she was lying' instead of 'He must have known she was lying'. The error arises because the two constructions sound alike when not emphasized.

off is liable to be misspelt as 'of'. Note 'run off', 'keep off the grass', 'take one's coat off', 'a house off the main street'. The spelling 'of' is totally wrong in phrases such as these. **Off** is used by some people instead of 'from', as in 'He bought the radio off a street trader'. This use should be avoided except in informal contexts.

offence is liable to be misspelt. Note the *c*. It is a common error to put *s* in the British English spelling. **Offense** is the standard American spelling.

officious and **official** are liable to be confused. They sound and look rather alike but they have different meanings. **Official** means 'authorized', as in 'receive an official pass to the conference' and 'The police have released an official statement', and 'formal', as in 'an official reception for the visiting diplomat'. **Officious** means 'too ready to give orders, offer advice, bossy, interfering, self-important', as in 'told by the officious woman behind the desk that I would have to provide other documenta-

tion' and 'The child who had lost the money for her fare
was put off the bus by an officious inspector'.

Oh *see* **O**.

OK and **okay** are both acceptable spellings of an informal word indicating agreement or approval, as in 'OK/
okay, I'll come with you', 'We've at last been given the
OK/okay to begin building'. When the word is used as a
verb it is more usually spelt **okay** because of the problem in adding endings, as in 'They've okayed our plans
at last'. **OK** is sometimes written with full stops as **O.K.**

older *see* **elder**.

omelette is frequently misspelt. Note the double *t* and first
e. This *e* is not sounded in the pronunciation. It is pronounced with the emphasis on the first syllable, as *om*-
lit. **Omelet** is the American English spelling.

omission is frequently misspelt. Note the single *m*. The
word means 'the act of leaving out', as in 'the acciden-
tal omission of his name from the list of invitations'.

one is used in formal situations to indicate an indefinite
person where 'you' would be used in informal situations,
as in 'One should not believe all one hears' and 'One
should be kind to animals'. This construction can sound
rather affected. Examples of the informal 'you' include
'You would've thought he would've had more sense'
and 'You wouldn't think anyone could be so stupid'. **One**
when followed by 'of the' and a plural noun takes a singular verb, as in 'One of the soldiers was killed' and
'One of the three witnesses has died'. However, the constructions 'one of those ... who' and one of the ... that'
take a plural verb, as in 'He is one of those people who

will not take advice' and 'It is one of those houses that are impossible to heat'.

only must be carefully positioned in written sentences to avoid confusion. It should be placed before, or as close as possible before, the word to which it refers. Compare 'She drinks only wine at the weekend', 'She drinks wine only at the weekend' and 'Only she drinks wine at the weekend'. In spoken English, where the intonation of the voice will indicate which word **only** applies to it may be placed in whichever position sounds most natural, usually between the subject and the verb, as in 'She only drinks wine at the weekend'.

onomatopoeia refers to 'the combination of sounds in a word that imitates or suggests the sound of what the word refers to'. 'Crackle', as in 'The fire crackled', 'hiss', as in 'The snake began to hiss', 'rumble', as in 'The thunder rumbled' are all examples of **onomatopoeia**. The word is frequently misspelt. Note the *oeia* combination.

onto and **on to** are both acceptable forms in sentences such as 'The cat leapt onto/on to the table' and 'He jumped from the plane onto/on to the ground'. However, in sentences such as 'It is time to move on to another city' **onto** is not a possible alternative'.

onward and onwards are not interchangeable. **Onward** is an adjective, as in 'onward motion' and 'onward progress'. **Onwards** is an adverb, as in 'march onwards' and 'proceed onwards'.

optician, ophthalmologist, optometrist and **oculist** all refer to 'a person who is concerned with disorders of the eyes' but they are not interchangeable. **Dispensing**

optician refers to 'a person who makes and sells spectacles or contact lenses'. **Ophthalmic optician** refers to 'a person who tests eyesight and prescribes lenses'. **Optometrist** is another term for this. **Ophthalmologist** refers to 'a doctor who specializes in disorders of the eyes' and **oculist** is another name for this. **Ophthalmologist** is frequently misspelt. Note the *h* after the *p*. It is pronounced of-thal-mol-*ol*-oj-ist.

optimum means 'the most favourable or advantageous condition, situation, amount, degree, etc', as in 'A temperature of 20° is optimum for these plants'. It is mostly used as an adjective meaning 'most favourable or advantageous', as in 'the optimum speed to run the car at', 'the optimum time at which to pick the fruit' and 'the optimum amount of water to give the plants'. It should not be used simply as a synonym for 'best'.

optometrist *see* **optician**.

or is accompanied by a singular verb when it connects singular subjects, as in 'Dessert will be ice cream or fruit salad' and 'Tuesday or Wednesday would be a suitable day'. A plural verb is used if the subjects are plural, as in 'Oranges or peaches are suitable' and 'Roses or carnations are possibilities'. If there is a combination of singular and plural subjects the verb agrees with the subject that is nearest to it, as in 'One very large cake or several small ones have been ordered' and 'Several small cakes or one very large one has been ordered'.

oral *see* **aural**.

orientate and **orient** are both acceptable forms of the same word. **Orientate** is the more common in British English

orthopaedic

but the shorter form, **orient**, is preferred by some people and is the standard form in American English. They are verbs meaning 'to get one's bearings', as in 'difficult to orientate/orient themselves in the mist on the mountain'; 'to adjust to new surroundings', as in 'It takes some time to orientate/orient oneself in a new job'; 'to direct at', as in 'The course is orientated/oriented at older students'; 'to direct the interest of to', as in 'try to orientate/orient students towards the sciences'.

orthopaedic and **paediatric** are liable to be confused. They both apply to medical specialties but they are different. **Orthopaedic** means 'referring to the treatment of disorders of the bones', as in 'attend the orthopaedic clinic with an injured back'. **Paediatric** means 'referring to the treatment of disorders associated with children', as in 'Her little boy is receiving treatment from a paediatric consultant'. In American English these are respectively spelt **orthopedic and pediatric**.

other than can be used when **other** is an adjective or pronoun, as in 'There was no means of entry other than through a trap door' and 'He disapproves of the actions of anyone other than himself'. Traditionally it should not be used as an adverbial phrase, as in 'It was impossible to get there other than by private car'. In such constructions **otherwise than** should be used, as in 'It is impossible to get there otherwise than by private car.' However, **other than** used adverbially is common in modern usage.

otherwise traditionally should not be used as an adjective or pronoun, as in 'Pack your clothes, clean or otherwise' and 'We are not discussing the advantages, or otherwise, of the scheme at this meeting'. It is an adverb, as in 'We are in favour of the project but he obviously thinks otherwise' and 'The hours are rather long but otherwise the job is fine'. *See* **other than.**

outdoor and **outdoors** are not interchangeable. **Outdoor** is an adjective, as in 'encourage the children to take part in outdoor activities' and 'have an outdoor party'. **Outdoors** is an adverb, as in 'children going outdoors to play' and 'hold the party outdoors'.

outrageous is liable to be misspelt. Note the *e*. The word means 'shocking, offensive', as in 'their outrageous behaviour at the church service', and 'unconventional', as in 'wearing outrageous hats'.

outward and **outwards** are not completely interchangeable. **Outward** is an adjective, as in 'the outward journey', but it is also a possible alternative to **outwards,** the adverb, as in 'toes turned outwards/outward.

owing to *see* **due to.**

P

p *see* **pence**.

pace is a Latin word adopted into English where it means 'with due respect to', usually preceding a statement of disagreement, as in 'Pace Robert Louis Stevenson, but I do not think it is better to travel hopefully than to arrive' and 'Pace your parents, but you might well find that school days are not the happiest days of your life'. It is used in formal, literary or facetious contexts and is pronounced *pah*-chay.

paediatric *see* **orthopaedic**.

palate, palette and **pallet** are liable to be confused. They sound alike but they have completely different meanings. **Palate** means either 'the top part of the inside of one's mouth', as in 'have a sore throat and palate' and 'a cleft palate', or 'sense of taste, the ability to distinguish one taste from another', as in 'Sweet things do not appeal to my palate' and 'His wine merchant complimented him on his palate'. **Palette** refers to 'the board on which an artist's colours are mixed', as in 'mix a beautiful shade of purple on his palette'. **Pallet** refers to a large platform for carrying or storing goods', as in 'put a pallet of books on the fork-lift truck', or 'a hard bed or straw mattress', as in 'wounded soldiers lying on pallets'.

panacea and **placebo** are liable to be confused. **Panacea** means 'a universal remedy for all ills and troubles', as in 'The new government does not have a panacea for the country's problems'. It is often used loosely to mean any remedy for any problem, as in 'She thinks that a holiday will be a panacea for his unhappiness'. **Panacea** is pronounced pan-a-*see*-a. **Placebo** refers to 'a supposed medication that is just a harmless substance given to a patient as part of a drugs trial etc', as in 'She was convinced the pills were curing her headaches but the doctor has prescribed her a placebo'. It is pronounced pla-*see*-bo.

panic causes spelling problems with reference to the past participle, past tense and present participle as **panicked** and **panicking**, as in 'They panicked when they smelt the smoke' and 'The panicking audience rushed for the exit'. Note also **panicky**, as in 'She got a bit panicky when she heard the footsteps behind her'.

paraffin is frequently misspelt. Note the single *r* and double *f*. The word refers to 'a type of oil used in heaters and lights', as in 'paraffin lamps'.

parallel is frequently misspelt. Note the single *r* and double *l* and single *l*. Note also that the *l* does not double in the past participle and present participle, as **paralleled** and **paralleling.** The word means 'of lines having the same distance between them at every point' and 'exactly corresponding', as in 'a parallel case'. As a verb it means 'to be equal to', as in 'His comparison has never been paralleled', and 'to be comparable to or similar to', as in 'His experience of the firm paralleled hers'.

paralyse

paralyse is frequently misspelt. Note the *yse* ending. In American English it is spelt **paralyze**. The word means 'to prevent from moving', as in 'The accident paralysed him from the waist down' and 'to prevent from functioning', as in 'The strike paralysed the factory for weeks'.

parameter is a mathematical term that is very loosely used in modern usage to mean 'limit, boundary, framework' or 'limiting feature or characteristic', as in 'work within the parameters of our budget and resources'. The word is over-used and should be avoided where possible. The emphasis is on the second syllable as par-*am*-it-er.

paranoid is an adjective meaning 'referring to a mental disorder, called **paranoia**, characterized by delusions of persecution and grandeur', as in 'a paranoid personality'. In modern usage it is used loosely to mean 'distrustful, suspicious of others, anxious etc', as in 'It is difficult to get to know him—he's so paranoid' and 'paranoid about people trying to get his job', when there is no question of actual mental disorder. **Paranoia** is pronounced par-a-*noy*-a.

paraphernalia means 'all the bits and pieces of equipment required for something', as in 'all the paraphernalia needed to take a baby on holiday', 'put his angling paraphernalia in the car'. Strictly speaking it is a plural noun but it is now frequently used with a singular verb, as in 'The artist's paraphernalia was lying all over the studio'. **Paraphernalia** is liable to be misspelt. Note the *er* before the *n*.

parentheses *see* **brackets**.

parliament is liable to be misspelt. Note the *i* before the *a*. It is pronounced *par*-la-ment. It refers to 'a legislative assembly or authority'. When it refers to a particular assembly, such as the British one, it is usually spelt with a capital letter.

parlour *see* **sitting room**.

particular means 'special, exceptional', as in 'a matter of particular importance', or 'individual', as in 'Have you a particular person in mind?', and 'concerned over details, fastidious', as in 'very particular about personal hygiene'. **Particular** is often used almost meaninglessly, as in 'this particular dress' and 'this particular car', when **particular** does not add much to the meaning.

partner can be used to indicate one half of an established couple, whether the couple are married or living together, as in 'Her partner was present at the birth of the child'.

passed and **past** are liable to be confused. **Passed** is the past participle and past tense of the verb 'to pass', as in 'She has already passed the exam' and 'They passed an old man on the way'. **Past** is used as a noun, as in 'He was a difficult teenager but that is all in the past now' and 'He has a murky past'. It is also used as an adjective, as in 'I haven't seen him in the past few weeks' and 'Her past experiences affected her opinion of men'. **Past** can also be a preposition, as in 'We drove past their new house', 'It's past three o'clock' and 'He's past caring'. It can also be an adverb, as in 'He watched the athletes running past' and 'The boat drifted past'.

patent, in British English, is usually pronounced *pay*-tent, as in 'patent leather dancing shoes'. **Patent** in the sense of 'obvious', as in 'his patent dislike of the situation' and 'It was quite patent that she loved him' is also pronounced in that way. **Patent** in the sense of 'a legal document giving the holder the sole right to make or sell something and preventing others from imitating it', as in 'take out a patent for his new invention', can be pronounced either *pay*-tent or *pat*-ent. **Patent** in this last sense can also be a verb, as in 'He should patent his invention as soon as possible'.

peaceable and **peaceful** are interchangeable in some meanings. Both **peaceable** and **peaceful** can mean 'not quarrelsome or aggressive, peace-loving', as in 'He is a peaceable person but his neighbours are always trying to pick a quarrel' and 'peaceful nations unwilling to go to war'. They can also both mean 'without fighting or disturbance, non-violent', as in 'try to reach a peaceable settlement' and 'take part in a peaceful demonstration'. **Peaceful** means 'characterized by peace, calm, quiet', as in 'a peaceful spot for a quiet holiday' and peaceful country scene'. **Peaceable** is frequently misspelt. Note the *e* before the second *a* and note the *-able*, not *-ible*, ending.

pedal and **peddle** are liable to be confused. They sound alike but have different meanings. **Pedal** refers to a 'foot-operated lever', as in 'The pedal on his bicycle broke' and 'the soft pedal on a piano'. It is also a verb meaning 'to operate a pedal', as in 'pedal the bicycle slowly uphill'. **Peddle** is a verb meaning 'to sell small articles from house to house or from place to place, to hawk', as in 'tinkers peddling clothes pegs and paper flowers around the village'. It also means 'to put forward or spread', as in 'peddle his agnostic theories'. In modern usage **peddle** is often used of selling drugs, as in 'evil men peddling hard drugs to young people'.

peddle *see* **pedal**.

peddler and **pedlar** are not interchangeable in British English. **Peddler** refers particularly to 'a person who peddles drugs', as in 'drug-peddlers convicted and sent to prison'. **Pedlar** refers to 'a person who sells small articles from house to house or from place to place', as in 'pedlars selling ribbons at the fair'.

pedlar *see* **peddler**.

pejorative is liable to be mispronounced. In modern usage it is pronounced with the emphasis on the second syllable, as in pi-*jor*-at-iv. It means 'expressing criticism or scorn, derogatory, disparaging', as in 'It was unsportsmanlike to make pejorative remarks about his rival'.

pence, p and **pennies** are liable to be confused. **Pence** is the plural form of 'penny', as in 'There are a hundred pence in the pound'. It is commonly found in prices, as in 'apples costing 10 pence each'. **Pence** has become much more common than 'pennies', which tends to be associated with pre-decimalization money (the British currency was decimalized in 1972), as in 'There were twelve pennies in one shilling'. **Pence** is sometimes used as though it were singular, as in 'have no one-pence pieces'. In informal contexts **p** is often used, as in 'Have you got a 10p (pronounced ten pee) piece' and 'Those chocolate bars are fifteen p'. **Pence** in compounds is not pronounced in the same way as pence was pronounced in compounds before decimalization. Such words as 'ten pence' are now pronounced *ten pens*, with equal emphasis on each word. In pre-decimalization days it was pronounced *ten*-pens, with the emphasis on the first word.

pennies *see* **pence**.

people is usually a plural noun and so takes a plural verb, as in 'The local people were annoyed at the stranger's behaviour' and 'People were being asked to leave'. In the sense of 'nation', 'race' or 'tribe' it is sometimes treated as a singular noun, as in 'the nomadic peoples of the world'. **People** acts as the plural of 'person', as in 'There's room for only one more person in that car but there's room for three people in this one'. In formal or legal contexts **persons** is sometimes used as the plural of 'person', as in 'The lift had a notice saying "Room for six persons only"'.

per means 'for each' and is used to express rates, prices, etc, as in 'driving at 60 miles per hour', 'cloth costing £5 per square metre', 'The cost of the trip is £20 per person' and 'The fees are £1000 a term per child'. It can also mean 'in each', as in 'The factory is inspected three times per year'.

per capita is a formal expression meaning 'for each person', as in 'The cost of the trip will be £300 per capita'. It is a Latin phrase which has been adopted into English and literally means 'by heads'. It is pronounced per *ka-pi-ta*.

per cent is usually written as two words. It is used adverbially in combination with a number in the sense of 'in or for each hundred', as in '30 per cent of the people are living below the poverty line'. The number is sometimes written in figures, as in 'Fifty per cent of the staff are married'. The symbol % is often used instead of the words 'per cent', especially in technical contexts, as in 'make savings of up to 30%'. **Per cent** in modern usage is sometimes used as a noun, as in 'They have agreed to lower the price by half a per cent'.

percentage refers to 'the rate, number or amount in each hundred', as in 'the number of unemployed people expressed as a percentage of the adult population' and 'What percentage of his salary is free?'. It is also used to mean proportion, as in 'Only a small percentage of last year's students have found jobs' and 'A large percentage of the workers are in favour of a strike' 'In modern usage it is sometimes used to mean 'a small amount' or 'a small part', as in 'Only a percentage of the students will find work'.

perceptible and **perceptive** are liable to be confused. They look and sound rather similar but they mean different things. **Perceptible** means 'noticeable, recognizable', as in 'There was no perceptible difference in her appearance even after all those years' and 'There has been a perceptible improvement in her work'. **Perceptive** means 'quick to notice and understand', as in 'She was perceptive enough to realize that she was not welcome, although her hosts tried to hide the fact', and 'having or showing understanding or insight, discerning', as in 'She wrote a perceptive analysis of his poetry'.

perpetrate and **perpetuate** are liable to be confused. **Perpetrate** means 'to commit, to perform', as in 'perpetrate a crime' and 'perpetrate an act of violence'. **Perpetuate**

perquisite

means 'to cause to continue', as in 'perpetuate the myth that women are helpless' and 'His behaviour will simply perpetuate his reputation as a villain'.

perquisite *see* **prerequisite.**

per se is a Latin phrase that has been adapted into English and means 'in itself', as in 'The substance is not per se harmful but it might be so if it interacts with other substances' and 'Television is not per se bad for children'. It should be used only in formal contexts.

persecute and **prosecute** are liable to be confused. They look and sound rather similar but they mean different things. **Persecute** means 'to treat cruelly, to oppress, to harass', as in 'The Christians in ancient Rome were persecuted for their beliefs' and 'Some of the pupils persecuted the new boy because he was so different from them'. **Prosecute** means 'to take legal action against', as in 'He was prosecuted for embezzling money from the company' and 'Shoplifters will be prosecuted'. It also means 'to follow, to continue to be occupied with', as in 'prosecute a new line of inquiry' and 'prosecute his musical career'. This meaning should be restricted to formal contexts.

person is now used in situations where 'man' was formerly used to avoid sexism in language'. It is used when the sex of the person being referred to is either unknown or not specified, as in 'They are advertising for another person for the warehouse'. It often sounds more natural to use 'someone', as in 'They are looking for someone to help out in the warehouse'. **Person** is often used in compounds, as in **chairperson, spokesperson** and **sales-**

person, although some people dislike this convention and some compounds, such as **craftsperson**, have not really caught on. **Person** has two possible plurals. *See* **people**. **Person with** and **people with** are phrases advocated in 'politically correct' language to avoid negative terms such as 'victim', 'sufferer', as in 'person with Aids'.

personal and **personnel** are liable to be confused. **Personal** is an adjective meaning 'of or affecting a person', as in 'carry out the scheme for personal gain' and 'her personal belongings'; 'of or belonging to a particular person rather than a group', as in 'state her personal opinion rather than the official company policy'; 'done in person', as in 'thanks to her personal intervention'; 'of the body', as in 'personal hygiene'; 'critical of a person's character, etc', as in 'upset by her personal remarks'. **Personnel** refers to 'the people employed in a workplace, such as an an office, shop, factory, etc, considered collectively', as in 'personnel officer, 'personnel department', 'Some of the local firms are beginning to recruit more personnel' and 'cut back on personnel during the recession'. It is rather a formal word and is best restricted to a business situation, such as recruitment advertisements. Words such as 'staff', 'workers' and 'employees' can be used instead. **Personnel** is liable to be misspelt. Note the double *n* and single *l*.

phase *see* **faze**.

phenomenal means 'referring to a phenomenon'. It is often used to mean 'remarkable, extraordinary', as in 'a phenomenal atmospheric occurrence', and in modern usage it is also used loosely to mean 'very great', as in 'a phenomenal increase in the crime rate' and 'a phenomenal achievement'. This use is usually restricted to informal contexts.

phenomenon is a singular noun meaning 'a fact, object, occurrence, experience, etc, that can be perceived by the senses rather than by thought or intuition', as in 'She saw something coming out of the lake but it remained an unexplained phenomenon', and 'a strange, unusual or remarkable fact, event or person of some particular significance', as in 'Single parenthood is one of the phenomena of the 1990s'. The plural is **phenomena**, as in 'natural phenomena'. It is a common error to treat **phenomena** as a singular noun. Note the spelling of **phenomenon** as it is liable to be misspelt.

phlegm causes problems with reference to both spelling and pronunciation. Note the *g*, which is often omitted in error. The word is pronounced *flem* and refers to 'a thick mucus secreted by respiratory passages, especially when one has a cold etc', as in 'cough up phlegm'. It also refers to 'slowness to act, react or feel, indifference', as in 'She seemed to face the crisis with an amazing amount of phlegm'. The adjective from this is phlegmatic, meaning 'slow to act, react or feel, indifferent, calm', as in 'require a phlegmatic temperament to cope with all the crises in the office'.

phobia refers to 'an abnormal or irrational fear or aversion', as in 'She is consulting a psychiatrist about her phobia about birds' and 'try to cure his phobia about flying'. It is often used loosely in modern usage to mean 'dislike', as in 'a phobia about people with red hair', or 'obsession', as in 'She has a phobia about her weight.' **Phobia** is liable to be misspelt. Note the *ph*.

phone, which is a short form of 'telephone', is not regarded as being as informal as it once was. It is quite acceptable in sentences such as 'He is going to buy a mobile phone', 'There is an extension phone in the kitchen'. It can also be used as a verb, as in 'Could you phone back tomorrow?' and 'Phone the doctor—it's an emergency'. Telephone is used only in very formal or official contexts', as in 'Please telephone for an application form'. 'If you wish to make an appointment with Mr Jones you will have to telephone his secretary'. Note that **phone** is now spelt without an apostrophe.

phoney and **phony** are both acceptable spellings but **phoney** is the more common in British English. The word means 'pretending or claiming to be what one is not, fake', as in 'He has a phoney American accent' and 'There's something phoney about him'.

photo is an abbreviation of 'photograph' which is usually used in an informal context, as in 'His mother is showing his girlfriend his baby photos', 'He's boring everybody with his holiday photos'. In more formal and official contexts 'photograph' is used, as in 'Assemble the children for the school photograph' and 'Enclose the photographs with the passport application form'. The plural of **photo** is **photos**. It is not generally used as a verb.

picnic causes problems with regard to the past participle, past tense and present participle. They add a *k* after the final *c* before the endings are added, as **picnicked** and **picnicking**, as in 'They picnicked by the river' and 'We were picnicking on wine'. Note also **picnicker**, as in 'Picnickers should not leave litter'.

pidgin and **pigeon** are liable to be confused. **Pidgin** refers to 'a language that is a mixture of two other languages', as in 'unable to understand the local people who were speaking pidgin English'. **Pigeon** is 'a type of bird of the dove family', as in 'pigeons eating crumbs as we were eating our sandwiches'.

pièce de résistance is a French phrase that has been adopted into English meaning 'the most important or impressive item', as in 'His portrait of his wife was the pièce de résistance of the exhibition'. The phrase is liable to be misspelt. Note the accent on the *e* of **pièce** which should not be omitted or it becomes 'piece'. Note also the accent on the first *e* of **résistance**. The phrase is pronounced pyes-de-re-*zist*-ahns.

pigeon *see* **pidgin**.

placebo *see* **panacea**.

plain and **plane** are liable to be confused since they sound alike. However, they have completely different meanings. **Plain** can be an adjective with several meanings. It means 'easy to see, hear or understand, clear', as in 'It was plain that she was unhappy' and 'speak in plain English so that you will be understood'; 'frank, not trying to deceive', as in 'the plain truth'; 'simple, not decorated or fancy', as in 'a plain style of dressing' and 'plain food'; 'without a pattern', as in 'prefer a plain material'; 'not beautiful', as in 'People said that she was the plain one of the family'. **Plain** as a noun refers to 'a large area of flat, treeless land', as in 'grow wheat on the plains'. **Plane** as a noun means 'the shortened form of aeroplane', as in 'Travelling by plane will be quicker'; 'a flat or level surface', as in 'create a plane by levelling the surface'; 'a level or standard', as in 'His mind is on a different plane from ours' and 'reach a higher plane of development'; 'a tool for smoothing surfaces', as in 'use a plane to smooth out the imperfections in the wood'. Note the **plain** in the phrase **plain sailing**, as in 'She thought it would be plain sailing once she got a place of her own but there were problems'. It is a common error to put **plane**. *See* **plane**.

plaintiff and **plaintive** are liable to be confused because they sound similar. However, they have completely different meanings. **Plaintiff** refers to 'a person who brings a legal action against someone', as in 'It was the accused's mother who was the plaintiff'. **Plaintive** means 'sounding sad, mournful', as in 'the plaintive cries of hungry children' and 'the plaintive sound of the bagpipes'.

plane and **aeroplane** mean the same thing, both referring to a 'a machine that can fly and is used to carry people and goods'. In modern usage **plane** is the usual term, as in 'The plane took off on time' and 'nearly miss the plane'. **Aeroplane** is slightly old-fashioned or unduly formal, as in 'Her elderly parents say that they refuse to travel by aeroplane'. The American English spelling is **airplane**. Note that **plane** is not spelt with an apostrophe although it is a shortened form. *See also* **plain**.

pleaded

pleaded and **pled** mean the same thing, both being the past tense and past participle of the verb 'to plead'. **Pleaded** is the usual form in British English, as in 'They pleaded with the tyrant to spare the child's life' and 'The accused was advised to plead guilty'. **Pled** is the usual American spelling.

plenty is used only informally in some contexts. It is acceptable in formal and informal contexts when it is followed by the preposition 'of', as in 'We have plenty of food', or when it is used as a pronoun without the 'of' construction, as in 'You can borrow some food from us—we have plenty'. Some people think its use as an adjective, as in 'Don't hurry—we have plenty time' and 'There's plenty food for all in the fridge', should be restricted to informal contexts. As an adverb it is acceptable in both formal and informal contexts in such sentences as 'Help yourself—we have plenty more'. However, such sentences as 'The house is plenty big enough for them' is suitable only for very informal or slang contexts'.

plurals cause many problems. Most words in English add *s* to form the plural, as in 'cats', 'machines' and 'boots'. However, words ending in -*s*, -*x*, -*z*, -*ch* and -*sh* add *es*, as in 'buses', 'masses', 'foxes', 'fezzes or fezes', 'churches' and 'sashes'. Nouns ending in a consonant followed by *y* have -*ies* in the plural, as 'fairies' and 'ladies', but note 'monkey', where the *y* is preceded by a vowel and becomes 'monkeys'. Proper nouns ending in *y* add *s*, as in 'the two Germanys'. Some words ending in *f* have *ves* in the plural, as 'wives' and 'halves', but some sim-

ply add s to the singular form, as 'beliefs'. Some words
ending in f can either add s or change to ves, as 'hoofs or
hooves'. Words ending in o cause problems as some end
in oes in the plural, as 'potatoes' and 'tomatoes', and
some end in s, as in 'pianos', while some can be spelt
either way and have to be learned or looked up in a dictionary etc. Shortened forms, such as 'photo' and 'vid-
eo', add simply s, as 'photos', 'videos'. Some words have
the same form in the plural as they do in the singular,
such as 'sheep' and 'deer'. Some are plural in form already and so do not change,. These include 'trousers'
and 'scissors'. Several words in English have irregular
plural forms which just have to be learned or looked up
in a dictionary, etc. These include 'men', 'mice' and
'feet'. Some foreign words adopted into English used to
retain the foreign plural form in English but this is becoming less common and, at the very least there is now
often an English-formed alternative, as 'gateaux/ga-
teaus', 'index/indices', 'formulae/formulas', 'appendix-
es/appendices'. However, several nouns of foreign ex-
traction retain the foreign-style plural in English, such
as 'criteria' and 'crises'.

p.m. *see* **a.m.**

poignant is liable to be misspelt. Note the *g*, which is
silent. It is pronounced *poy*-nyant. The word means 'affecting one's feelings deeply, distressing', as in 'a poignant tale of an orphan child'.

politic and **political** are liable to be confused although
they are completely different in meaning. **Politic** means
'prudent, wise', as in 'He thought it politic not to men-

tion that he knew that his boss had been fined for speed-
ing'. **Political** means 'referring to politics', as in 'political parties' and 'the end of his political career'. **Politic**
is pronounced with the emphasis on the first syllable, as
pol-it-ik, but **political** is pronounced with the emphasis
on the second syllable as pol-*it*-ic-al.

political correctness is a modern movement aiming to
remove all forms of prejudice in language, such as sexism, racism and discrimination against disabled people.
Its aims are admirable but in practice many of the words
and phrases suggested by advocates of political correctness are rather contrived or, indeed, ludicrous. The adjective is **politically correct**.

pore and **pour** are liable to be confused because they sound
alike. **Pore** as a verb means 'to look at or study intent-
ly', as in 'They pored over the old document looking for
the site of the treasure'. **Pour** means 'to cause to flow',
as in 'she poured milk from the jug', or 'to flow in large
amounts', as in 'Water poured from the burst pipe'. **Pore**
can also be a noun when it means 'one of the tiny open-
ings on the surface of the skin', as in 'clogged pores'.

portrait is liable to be misspelt. Note the first *r*. The word
means 'a painting, drawing or photograpgh of a person
or animal, particularly one which concentrates on the
face', as in 'portraits of his ancestors hanging on the
walls of the dining room'.

portray is liable to be misspelt. Note the first *r*. It means
'to paint or draw', as in 'The queen was portrayed in her
coronation robes'; 'to describe', as in 'In his autobiog-
raphy his father is portrayed as a bully'; 'and to act the

part of', as in 'The actress portrayed Desdemona in *Othello*'.

Portuguese is liable to be misspelt. Note the *u* after the *g*. It is the adjective from 'Portugal'.

possessives are indicated in English by either apostrophes or the preposition 'of', as in 'the boy's books', Jim's car', the dogs' kennels', 'the key of the back door' and 'The soldiers of the king'. When the 'of' construction is used of people, an apostrophe is often used as well, as in 'a colleague of her husband's'. The 'of' construction is usually used of things rather than people, as in 'The catch of the garden gate is broken', and it is usually used when geographical regions are being referred to, as in 'the forests of Scandinavia'. If the possession in question refers to more than one person the apostrophe goes on the last owner mentioned, as in 'John and Mary's beautiful house'. In the case of compound nouns, the apostrophe goes on the last word, as in 'the lady-in-waiting's role'. For the position of the apostrophe in **possessives** *see* **apostrophe**.

posthumous causes problems with both spelling and pronunciation. Note the *h*, which is often omitted in error since it is silent in pronunciation. The word is pronounced *post*-ewmus with the emphasis on the first syllable, which rhymes with 'lost'. The word means 'happening or given after death', as in 'a posthumous novel' and 'a posthumous medal'. The adverb **posthumously** means 'after one's death', as in 'The soldier's son was born posthumously'.

pour *see* **pore**.

practicable

practicable and **practical** should not be used interchangeably. **Practicable** means 'able to be done or carried
out, able to be put into practice', as in 'His schemes seem
fine in theory but they are never practicable'. **Practical**
has several meanings, such as 'concerned with action
and practice rather than with theory', as in 'He has stud-
ied the theory but has no practical experience of the job';
'suitable for the purpose for which it was made', as in
'practical shoes for walking'; 'useful', as in 'a practical
device with a wide range of uses'; 'clever at doing and
making things', as in 'She's very practical when it comes
to dealing with an emergency'; 'virtual', as in 'He's not
the owner but he's in practical control of the firm'.

practically can mean 'in a practical way', as in 'Practically, the scheme is not really possible', but in modern
usage it is usually used to mean 'virtually', as in 'He
practically runs the firm although he is not the manager', and 'almost', as in 'The driver of that car practically
ran me over'.

practice and **practise** are not interchangeable. **Practice**
is a noun, as in 'She has gone to netball practice', 'It is
time to put the plan into practice', 'It is accepted practice to tip the waiters', 'object to some of the practices
of the religious sect' and 'Our doctor has retired from
the practice'. **Practise** is the verb form, as in 'He practises the piano every evening', 'We must practise economy if we are to remain solvent', 'He is a medical doctor but he has not practised for years' and 'He is a Catholic but he no longer practises his religion'. Note that
practise is not one of the verbs that can end in *-ize*. In

American English both the noun and the verb are spelt **practice**.

pray and **prey** are liable to be confused. They sound alike but they have completely different meanings. **Pray** means 'to speak to God, to make requests of God', as in 'pray and sing hymns in church on Sundays' and 'pray to God that the pardon will arrive in time', or 'to ask a favour from, to beg', as in 'They prayed to the tyrant to release their brother'. **Prey** is a noun meaning 'an animal or bird hunted and killed by another animal or bird', as in 'The lion had its prey, a deer, in its mouth'. It also means 'a person who is exploited or harmed by another, a victim', as in 'The old lady was easy prey for the con man'. **Prey** is also a verb meaning 'to hunt and kill as prey', as in 'Eagles prey on small animals', and 'to trouble greatly, to obsess', as in 'His part in the crime preyed on his mind'.

precede and **proceed** are liable to be confused because they sound alike but they mean different things. **Precede** means 'to go in front of', as in 'The guide preceded us into the room', 'to come in front of', as in 'The text is preceded by a long introduction' and 'He preceded her as chairman'. **Proceed** means 'to go on, to continue', as in 'Work is proceeding at an even pace' and 'We were told to proceed with our work', or 'to make one's way, to go', as in 'They were proceeding up the street in a drunken manner'.

precipitate and **precipitous** are liable to be confused. **Precipitate** as an adjective means 'violently hurried', as in 'When the thief saw the policeman he made a pre-

prefer

cipitate dash from the room', 'sudden', as in 'Her precipitate disappearance from the firm', and 'rash, impul-
sive', as in 'We thought his action in leaving the firm
was rather precipitate'. **Precipitous** means 'very steep,
like a precipice', as in 'It was almost impossible to climb
the precipitous slope'. **Precipitate** is also a verb meaning to cause something to happen suddenly or sooner
than expected, to hasten', as in 'His setting fire to the
bicycle shed precipitated his expulsion from the school',
or 'to throw', as in 'His sudden departure precipitated
the whole office into a state of confusion'. In the pronunciation of both the verb and the adjective, the emphasis is on the second syllable, but in the case of the
verb the last syllable rhymes with 'gate' whereas in the
case of the adjective the last syllable is pronounced to
rhyme with 'hat'. Thus the pronunciation of the adjective is pri-*sip*-i-tat, and that of the verb pri-sip-it-ayt.

prefer is followed by the preposition 'to' not 'than', as in
'She prefers dogs to cats', 'They prefer Paris to London' and 'They prefer driving to walking'. **Prefer** causes spelling problems with regard to the past participle,
past tense and present participle. Note that the final *r* of
prefer doubles before the '-ed' and '-ing' are added, as
preferred and **preferring**. The word means 'to like better', as in 'She preferred the country to the town'.

premier and **première** are liable to be confused. **Premier**
means 'leading, principle', as in 'He is the premier authority on genetic engineering in the country'. **Première**
refers to 'the first performance of a film, play, etc', as in
'attend the world première of his latest film'. It is now

212

also a verb, as in 'His latest film was premiered in London'. **Premier** is pronounced *prem*-ier. Première is pronounced *prem*-i-ay or *prem*-i-ayr. **Première** is liable to be misspelt. Note the final *e*. The word is usually spelt with a grave accent over the second *e*.

premise *see* **premises**.

premises and **premise**. are liable to be confused. **Premises** refers to 'a building including any outbuildings and grounds', as in 'the car sales showroom has moved to new premises'. **Premises** is a plural noun and so takes a plural verb, as in 'Their present premises are too small for the volume of business'. **Premise** is a singular noun meaning 'assumption, hypothesis', as in 'His advice was based on the premise that they had enough capital for the project'. It is also spelt **premiss**.

premiss *see* **premises**.

prerequisite and **perquisite** are liable to be confused although they are completely different in meaning. **Perquisite** means 'money or goods given as a right in addition to one's pay', as in 'various perquisites such as a company car'. It is frequently abbreviated to 'perks', as in 'The pay's not very much but the perks are good'. **Prerequisite** refers to 'something required as a condition for something to happen or exist', as in 'Passing the exam is a prerequisite for his getting the job' and 'A certain amount of studying is a prerequisite of passing the exam'.

prescribe and **proscribe** are liable to be confused. They sound similar but are completely different in meaning. **Prescribe** means 'to advise or order the use of, espe-

prestige

cially a medicine or remedy', as in 'The doctor prescribed antibiotics' and 'The doctor prescribed complete bed rest'. It also means 'to lay down as a rule or law', as in 'School regulations prescribe that all pupils wear school uniform'. **Proscribe** means 'to prohibit', as in 'proscribe the carrying of guns', and 'to outlaw or exile', as in 'proscribe the members of the clan who betrayed the chief'. In some cases the words are virtually opposite in meaning. Compare 'The lecturer has prescribed several books which must be read by the end of term' and 'The government has proscribed several books that are critical of them'.

prestige is liable to be mispronounced. It is pronounced prez-*teezh* and means 'the respect, status or renown derived from achievement, distinction, wealth, glamour etc', as in 'He suffered a loss of prestige when he lost all his money' and 'He enjoys the prestige of being chairman of the company'.

prevaricate and **procrastinate** are liable to be confused although they have completely different meanings. **Prevaricate** means 'to try to avoid telling the truth by speaking in an evasive or misleading way', as in 'She prevaricated when the police asked her where she had been the previous evening'. **Procrastinate** means 'to delay or postpone action', as in 'The student has been procrastinating all term but now he has to get to grips with his essay'.

preventative and **preventive** both mean 'preventing or intended to prevent, precautionary', as in 'If you think the staff are stealing from the factory you should take

214

preventative/preventive measures' and 'Preventative/preventive medicine seeks to prevent disease and disorders rather than cure them'. **Preventive** is the more frequently used of the two terms.

prey *see* **pray**.

prima facie is a Latin phrase that has been adopted into English. It means 'at first sight, based on what seems to be so' and is mainly used in legal or very formal contexts, as in 'The police say they have prima facie evidence for arresting him but more investigation is required'. The phrase is pronounced *pri*-ma *fay*-shee.

primarily is traditionally pronounced with the emphasis on the first syllable, as *prim*-ar-el-i. Since this is difficult to say unless one is speaking very slowly and carefully, it is becoming increasingly common to pronounce it with the emphasis on the second syllable, as prim-*err*-el-i. It means 'mainly', as in 'He was primarily interested in the creative side of the business' and 'The course is primarily a practical one'.

primeval and **primaeval** are both acceptable forms of the word meaning 'of the earliest period in the history of the world, very ancient', as in 'primeval rocks'. In modern usage **primeval** is the more common term although **primaeval** was formerly the more usual term.

principal and **principle** are liable to be confused. They sound alike but they have different meanings. **Principal** means 'chief, main', as in 'his principal reason for leaving' and 'her principal source of income'. **Principal** is also a noun meaning 'head', as in 'the principal of the college'. **Principle** means 'a basic general truth', as in 'accord-

principle

ing to scientific principles', and 'a guiding rule for personal behaviour', as in 'It is against his principles to lie'.

principle *see* **principal**.

prise and **prize** are liable to cause confusion. The verb 'to force open' can be spelt either **prise** or **prize**, as in 'prise/prize open the chest with an iron bar'. **Prise** is the more common spelling. **Prize** has another meaning for which prise cannot be substituted. It means 'an award or reward', as in 'He won first prize in the tennis competition', and 'something won in a lottery etc', as in 'He won first prize on the football pools'. **Prize** can also be a verb meaning 'to value highly', as in 'She prizes her privacy'.

privilege is liable to be misspelt. Note the *i* before the *l*, and the *e* before the *g*. It refers to 'a special right or advantage', as in 'the privileges conferred on ambassadors' and 'enjoy the privileges of being a senior executive'.

procrastinate *see* **prevaricate**.

professor is liable to be misspelt. Note the single *f* and the double *s*. The word means 'a senior university lecturer', as in 'The professor is retiring from the chair of English this year'.

prognosis *see* **diagnosis**.

programme and **program** are liable to cause confusion. In British English **programme** is the acceptable spelling in such senses as in 'a television programme', 'put on a varied programme of entertainment' 'buy a theatre programme' and 'launch an ambitious programme of expansion'. However, in the computing sense **program**

216

is used. **Programme** can also be a verb meaning 'to plan, to schedule', as in 'programme the trip for tomorrow'; 'to cause something to conform to a particular set of instructions', as in 'programme the central heating system'; or 'to cause someone to behave in a particular way, especially to conform to particular instructions', as in 'Her parents have programmed her to obey them implicitly'. In the computing sense of 'to provide with a series of coded instructions', the verb is spelt **program** and the *m* is doubled to form the past participle, past tense and present participle, as **programmed** and **programming**. In American English **program** is the accepted spelling for all senses of both noun and verb.

prophecy and **prophesy** are liable to confused. **Prophecy** is a noun meaning 'prediction', as in 'Some of the old woman's prophecies came true'. **Prophesy** is a verb meaning 'to predict', as in 'The old woman had prophesied the disaster that befell the village' and 'They prophesied that the recession would be over in a year'. **Prophecy** is pronounced with the emphasis on the first syllable, as *pro*-fi-si. **Prophesy** is also pronounced with the emphasis on the first syllable, but the last syllable rhymes with 'eye' as *pro*-fi-si.

proscribe *see* **prescribe**.

prosecute *see* **persecute**.

prostate and **prostrate** are liable to be confused although they are completely different in meaning. **Prostate** refers to 'a gland around the neck of the bladder in men', as in 'have a prostate complaint' and 'contract cancer of the prostate'. **Prostrate** means 'lying face downwards',

protagonist

as in 'The injured rider was lying prostrate on the ground', 'overcome by', as in 'prostrate with grief', and 'exhausted, helpless', as in 'a country competely prostrate after the war'. **Prostrate** is also a verb meaning 'to throw oneself face down on the ground, for example, as a sign of submission', as in 'The soldiers prostrated themselves before the emperor', 'to overcome', as in 'Grief prostrated her', and 'to make helpless or exhausted', as in 'prostrated following a bout of flu'.

protagonist was originally a term for 'the chief character in a drama', as in 'Hamlet is the protagonist in the play that bears his name'. It then came to mean also 'the leading person or paticipant in an event, dispute, etc', as in 'The protagonists on each side of the dispute had a meeting'. In modern usage it can now also mean 'a leading or notable supporter of a cause, movement, etc,'as in 'She was one of the protagonists of the feminist movement'.

protein is liable to be misspelt. Note the *ei* combination. It is an exception to the 'i before e' rule. **Protein** refers to 'a substance that is an important body-building part of the diet of humans and animals', as in 'Meat, eggs and fish are sources of protein'.

provided and **providing** are used interchangeably, as in 'You may go, provided/providing that you have finished your work' and 'He can borrow the car provided/providing he pays for the petrol'. 'That' is optional. The phrases mean 'on the condition that'.

psychiatry is liable to be misspelt. Note the initial *p* and the *y* after the *s*. It is pronounced si-*ki*-i-tri and refers to 'the branch of medicine that deals with disorders of the mind'.

publicly is liable to be misspelt. There is no *k* before the *l*. It is a common error to spell it 'publically'. The word means 'not in private, in front of other people', as in 'He publicly admitted that he was at fault'.

pudding *see* **dessert.**

pupil and **student** are not interchangeable. **Pupil** refers to 'a child or young person who is at school', as in 'primary school pupils and secondary school pupils', **Student** refers to 'a person who is studying at a place of further education, at a university or college', as in 'students trying to find work during the vacations'. In modern usage senior **pupils** at secondary school are sometimes known as **students**. In American English student refers to people at school as well as to people in further education. **Pupil** can also refer to 'a person who is receiving instruction in something from an expert' as in 'The piano teacher has several adult pupils'. **Student** can also refer to 'a person who is studying a particular thing', as in 'In his leisure time he is a student of local history'.

purposefully and **purposely** are not interchangeable. **Purposefully** means 'determinedly', as in 'He strode purposefully up to the front of the hall and addressed the meeting'. **Purposely** means 'on purpose, deliberately', as in 'He didn't leave his book behind by accident—he did it purposely'.

Q

quasi- is Latin in origin and means 'as if, as it were'. In English it is combined with adjectives in the sense of 'seemingly, apparently, but not really', as in 'He gave a quasi-scientific explanation of the occurrence which convinced many people but did not fool his colleagues', or 'partly, to a certain extent but not completely', as in 'It is a quasi-official body which does not have full powers'. **Quasi-** can also be combined with nouns to mean 'seeming, but not really', as in 'a quasi-socialist who is really a capitalist' and 'a quasi-Christian who will not give donations to charity'. **Quasi-** has several possible pronunciations. It can be pronounced *kway*-zi, *kway*-si or *kwah*-si

quay is liable to be mispronounced. The spelling of the word does not suggest the pronunciation, which is *key*. It means 'a landing place', as in 'ships unloading at the quay'.

queer in the sense of 'homosexual' was formerly used only in a slang and derogatory or offensive way. However, it is now used in a non-offensive way by homosexual people to describe themselves, as an alternative to 'gay'.

question *see* **beg the question; leading question.**

questionnaire is liable to be misspelt. Note the double *n*.

Formerly the acceptable pronunciation was kes-tyon-*air*, but in modern usage kwes-chon-*air* is more common. The word refers to 'a list of questions to be answered by a number of people as part of a survey or collection of statistics', as in 'People entering the supermarket were asked to fill in a questionnaire on their shopping habits' and 'Householders were asked to complete a questionnaire on their electrical equipment'.

quick is an adjective meaning 'fast, rapid', as in 'a quick method', 'a quick route' and 'a quick walker'. It should not be used as an adverb, as in 'Come quick', in formal contexts since this is grammatically wrong.

quite has two possible meanings when used with adjectives. It can mean 'fairly, rather, somewhat', as in 'She's quite good at tennis but not good enough to play in the team' and 'The house is quite nice but it's not what we're looking for'. Where the indefinite article is used, **quite** precedes it, as in 'quite a good player' and 'quite a nice house'. '**Quite** can also mean 'completely, totally', as in 'We were quite overwhelmed by their generosity' and 'It is quite impossible for him to attend the meeting'.

R

rack and **wrack** are liable to be confused. **Rack** refers to
'a framework for storing and displaying things', as in 'a
luggage rack' and 'a vegetable rack'. It is also the name
given historically to an instrument of torture, consisting
of a frame on which a person lay with wrists and ankles
tied and had their arms stretched in one direction and
their legs in the other, as in 'prisoners on the rack'. The
verb **rack** means 'to cause to suffer pain or great distress to', as in 'cancer patients racked with agony',
'racked with uncertainty' and 'nerve-racking'. The
phrase 'rack one's brains' means 'to try hard to think of
or remember', as in 'racking his brains to remember their
address'. **Wrack** is a rarer word that refers to 'a kind of
seaweed' or 'a remnant of something that has been de-
stroyed'. **Rack** and **wrack** are interchangeable in the
phrase **rack/wrack and ruin**—'neglect, decay, destruc-
tion', as in 'Since the owner has been ill the business
has gone to rack/wrack and ruin'.

racket and **racquet** are liable to be confused. Either **racket**
or **racquet** may be used to indicate 'a kind of imple-
ment with a stringed frame used in sport for striking the
ball', as in 'tennis racket/racquet' and 'badminton rack-
et/racquet'. **Racket** also means 'a loud noise', as in
'neighbours complaining about the racket made by the

party guests' and 'children making a racket running up
and down stairs'. **Racket** also refers to 'a dishonest or
illegal way of making money', as in 'a drug racket' and
'a racket involving forged currency'.

raise and **raze** are liable to be confused. They sound alike
but have completely different meanings. **Raise** means
'to move to a higher position', as in 'raise the flag', 'raise
prices' and 'raise morale'. **Raze** means 'to destroy completely', as in 'The invading army razed the village to
the ground'.

raison d'être is French in origin and is used in English to
mean 'a reason, a justification for the existence of', as
in 'Her children are her raison d'être' and 'His only raison d'être is his work'. The phrase is liable to be misspelt. Note the accent (^) on the first *e*. It is pronounced
ray-zon detr.

rang and **rung** are liable to be confused. **Rang** is the past
tense of the verb 'to ring', as in 'She rang the bell', and
rung is the past participle, as in 'They had rung the bell'.

rara avis is French in origin and means literally 'rare bird'.
In English it is used to refer to 'a rare or unusual person
or thing', as in 'a person with such dedication to a company is a rara avis'. It is pronounced *ray*-ra *ayv*-is or *ra*-
ra *ay*-vis.

ravage and **ravish** are liable to be confused. They sound
rather similar although they have different meanings.
Ravage means 'to cause great damage to, to devastate',
as in 'low-lying areas ravaged by floods' and 'a population ravaged by disease', or 'to plunder, to rob', as in
'neighbouring tribes ravaging their territory'. **Ravish**

raze

    means either 'to delight greatly, to enchant', as in 'The audience were ravished by the singer's performance'. It also means 'to rape', as in 'The girl was ravished by her kidnappers', but this meaning is rather old-fashioned and is found only in formal or literary contexts.

raze *see* **raise.**

re, meaning 'concerning, with reference to', as in 'Re your correspondence of 26 November', should be restricted to business or formal contexts.

re- is a common prefix, meaning 'again', in verbs. In most cases it is not followed by a hyphen, as in 'retrace one's footsteps', 'a retrial ordered by the judge' and 'reconsider his decision'. However, it should be followed by a hyphen if its absence is likely to lead to confusion with another word, as in 're-cover a chair'/'recover from an illness', 're-count the votes'/'recount a tale of woe', 'the re-creation of a 17th-century village for a film set'/'play tennis for recreation' and 're-form the group'/'reform the prison system'. In cases where the second element of a word begins with *e*, **re-** is traditionally followed by a hyphen, as in 're-educate', re-entry' and 're-echo', but in modern usage the hyphen is frequently omitted.

readable *see* **legible.**

receipt is frequently misspelt. Note the *ei* combination in line with the '*i* before *e* except after *c*' rule. Note also *p*, which is not pronounced. **Receipt** is pronounced ri-*seet* and means either 'the act of receiving', as in 'on receipt of your letter', or 'a written statement that money, goods, etc, have been received', as in 'Keep the receipt in case you want to return the goods'.

recommend is frequently misspelt. Note the single *c* and double *m*. The word means 'to suggest as suitable, to praise as suitable', as in 'I can thoroughly recommend this brand of face cream', and 'to suggest as advisable, to advise', as in 'He recommends that we reduce expenditure'.

reconnaissance is frequently misspelt. Note the single *c*, double *n*, and double *s*. It is pronounced ri-*kon*-i-sins and means 'an exploration or survey of an area', as in 'troops engaged in reconnaissance' and 'undertake an aerial reconnaissance of the area where the child was lost'.

re-cover, recover *see* **re-**.

re-creation, recreation *see* **re-**.

refer causes problems with regard to its past participle, past tense and present participle. The *r* doubles before the addition of '-ed' or '-ing', as **referred** and **referring**, as in 'He referred to her good work in his speech' and 'He was not referring to the present holder of the post'. Note, however, **reference** with a single *r*.

referendum causes problems with regard to its plural form. It has two possible plural forms, **referendums** or **referenda**. In modern usage **referendums** is the more usual plural. **Referendum** means 'the referring of an issue of public importance to a general vote by all the people of a country', as in 'hold a referendum on whether to join the EC'.

re-form, reform *see* **re-**.

refrigerator is frequently misspelt. Note the *-or* ending, the *er* in the middle and the absence of *d*. It is a common error to include a *d* because of confusion with 'fridge'.

registry office and **register office** are interchangeable, although **registry office** is the more common term in general usage. The words refer to 'an office where civil marriage ceremonies are performed and where births, marriages and deaths are recorded', as in 'She wanted to be married in church but he preferred a registry office ceremony' and 'register the child's birth at the local registry office'.

reign and **rein** are liable to be confused. **Reign** is the time during which a king or queen reigns', as in 'during the reign of George V'. **Rein** refers to 'one of the leather straps that control a horse', as in 'The coachman let go of the reins and the horse bolted'. **Reins**, the plural of **rein**, refers to 'a means of control or restraint', as in 'The deputy president held the reins of power'. Both **reign** and **rein** can also be verbs. **Reign** means 'to rule as king or queen', as in 'a monarch who reigned for more than fifty years'. **Rein** as a verb is found in the phrase **rein in**, meaning 'to restrain or stop', as in 'rein in the horse'.

relevant is liable to be misspelt. Note the *-ant* ending. It means 'connected with what is being discussed, happening, done, etc', as in 'collect all the relevant information' and 'police noting details relevant to the case'.

reminiscences is frequently misspelt. Note the *sc* combination. The word refers to 'remembered experiences', as in 'listening to the old woman's reminiscences of her childhood days'. **Reminiscent** is an adjective meaning either 'thinking or talking about past events', as in 'in reminiscent mood', or 'reminding one of, suggesting

226

someone or something', as in 'The style of the artist is reminiscent of Monet'.

requisite *see* **perquisite.**

rhyme and **rime** are liable to be confused. They sound alike but have completely different meanings. **Rhyme** refers to 'a word which is like another in its final sound', as in 'tailor and sailor are rhymes', 'rough and puff are rhymes' and 'dilatory and military are rhymes'. **Rhyme** can also be a verb, as in 'tailor rhymes with sailor'. **Rime** refers to 'a thick white frost', as in 'fields covered with rime'.

rhythm is frequently misspelt. Note the first *h* and the *y*. It means 'a regular repeated pattern of sounds or beats', as in 'the fast rhythm of the dance music'.

rigorous is frequently misspelt. Note the absence of *u* before the second *r*. It is unlike **rigour** in this respect. **Rigorous** means 'severe, strict', as in 'the rigorous discipline of the army', 'harsh, unpleasant', as in 'rigorous weather conditions', and 'strict, detailed', as in 'with rigorous attention to the small print of the agreement'.

rigour and **rigor** are liable to be confused. They look similar but they have completely different meanings. **Rigour** means 'severity, strictness', as in 'the rigour of the punishment', and 'harshness, unpleasantness', as in 'the rigour of the climate' (in this sense it is often in the plural, **rigours**), and 'strictness, detailedness', as in 'the rigour of the editing'. **Rigor** is a medical term meaning 'rigidity', as in 'muscles affected by rigor', or 'a feeling of chilliness often accompanied by feverishness', as in 'infectious diseases of which rigor is one of the symp-

role

toms'. **Rigor** is also short for **rigor mortis**, meaning 'the stiffening of the body that occurs after death'. The first syllable of **rigour** is pronounced to rhyme with 'big', but **rigor** can be pronounced either in this way or with the *i* pronounced as in 'ride'

role can be spelt either with a circumflex, as **rôle**, or not, as **role**. **Role** is the more common spelling in modern usage. The word means 'part', as in 'play the role of Hamlet' and 'She had to play the role of mother and of father.' It can also be used to mean 'function, position', as in 'the role of play in a child's development'.

roof causes problems with regard to its plural form. The usual plural is **roofs**, which can be pronounced either as it is spelt, to rhyme with 'hoofs', or to rhyme with 'hooves'.

rout and **route** are liable to be confused. They look similar but are pronounced differently and have completely different meanings'. **Rout** as a noun means 'overwhelming defeat', as in 'the rout of the opposing army', and as a verb 'to defeat utterly', as in 'Their team routed ours last time'. **Route** refers to 'a way of getting somewhere', as in 'the quickest route' and 'the scenic route'. **Route** can also be a verb meaning 'to arrange a route for, to send by a certain route', as in 'route the visitors along the banks of the river'. **Rout** is pronounced to rhyme with 'shout'. **Route** is pronounced to rhyme with 'brute'.

rug *see* **carpet**.

rung *see* **rang**.

S

's and s' *see* **apostrophe**.

sacrilegious is frequently misspelt. Note the *i* before the *l* and the *e* before the g. It is a common error to confuse it with the pattern of 'religious'. **Sacrilegious** is the adjective from 'sacrilege' and means 'showing disrespect for something holy', as in 'the sacrilegious act of destroying the altar'.

salon and **saloon** are liable to be confused. **Salon** in modern usage is most frequently found as a name given to certain businesses, as 'own a hairdressing salon' and 'visit a beauty salon'. Formerly it was used to refer to a room in a large house where guests were received and also to 'a regular gathering of notable guests at the house of a noble lady or wealthy lady', as in 'hold a literary salon'.

sank, **sunk** and **sunken** are liable to be confused. **Sank** is the past tense of the verb 'to sink', as in 'The ship sank without trace'. **Sunk** is also used in this sense, as in 'The dog sunk its teeth into the postman's leg', but **sank** is the more common form. The past participle of 'sink' is **sunk**, as in 'We have sunk all our money in the business'. **Sunken** is a form of the past participle usually used as an adjective, as in 'sunken treasure' and 'sunken cheeks'.

scarfs

scarfs and **scarves** are both acceptable spellings of the plural of 'scarf', meaning a piece of cloth worn around the neck or the head', as in 'a silk scarf at her neck' and 'wearing a head scarf'.

sceptic and **septic** are liable to be confused, particularly with regard to their pronunciation. **Sceptic** is pronounced *skep*-tik and refers to 'a person who has doubts about accepted beliefs, principles, etc', as in 'The rest of the family are deeply religious but he is a sceptic'. **Septic** is pronounced *sep*-tik and means 'infected with harmful bacteria', as in 'a wound that turned septic' and 'have a septic finger'.

schedule, meaning 'plan or timetable', as in 'work that is behind schedule' and 'try to work out a revision schedule well before the exams', is usually pronounced *shed*-yool in British English. However, the American English pronunciation *sked*-yool is now sometimes found in British usage.

Scotch, Scots and **Scottish** are liable to be confused. **Scotch** is restricted to a few set phrases, such as 'Scotch whisky', 'Scotch broth' and 'Scotch mist'. As a noun **Scotch** refers to 'Scotch whisky', as in 'have a large Scotch with ice'. **Scots** as an adjective is used in such contexts as 'Scots accents', 'Scots people' and 'Scots attitudes'. As a noun **Scots** refers to the Scots language, as in 'He speaks standard English but he uses a few words of Scots.' The noun **Scot** is used to refer to 'a Scottish person', as in 'Scots living in London'. **Scottish** is found in such contexts as 'Scottish literature', 'Scottish history' and 'Scottish culture'.

sculpt and **sculpture** are interchangeable as verbs meaning 'to make sculptures, to practise sculpting', as in 'commissioned to sculpt/sculpture a bust of the chairman of the firm' and 'She both paints and sculpts/sculptures.

seasonal and **seasonable** are liable to be confused. They are both adjectives formed from the noun 'season' but they have different meanings. **Seasonal** means 'happening during a particular season, varying with the seasons', as in 'Hotel work is often seasonal' and 'a recipe that uses seasonal vegetables'. **Seasonable** means 'suitable for or appropriate to', as in 'seasonable weather'.

start *see* **commence**.

secretary is liable to be misspelt. Note the *-ary* ending. It is pronounced *sek*-re-tri and refers to 'a person employed to deal with correspondence, typing, filing, making appointments, etc', as in 'Her secretary is dealing with all her phone calls today'. It also refers to 'a person appointed in a society, club, etc, to deal with correspondence, take minutes, keep records, etc, as in 'elected secretary of tennis club'.

seize, meaning 'to take hold of suddenly and by force, to grab', as in 'The kidnappers seized the child' and 'seize the opportunity to escape', is frequently misspelt. Note the *ei* combination, which is an exception to the '*i* before *e* except after *c*' rule.

sensual and **sensuous** are liable to be confused. **Sensual** means 'relating to physical (often sexual) pleasure, enjoying or giving physical pleasure', as in 'the sensual pleasures of eating and drinking'. **Sensuous** means 'relating to the senses, giving pleasure to the senses', as in

sentiment

'the sensuous feel of silk' and 'the sensuous appeal of the music'.

sentiment and **sentimentality** are liable to be confused. They are related but have different shades of meaning. **Sentiment** means 'feeling, emotion', as in 'His actions were the result of sentiment not rationality'. It also means 'attitude, opinion', as in 'a speech full of anti-Christian sentiments'. **Sentimentality** is the noun from the adjective **sentimental** and means 'over-indulgence in tender feelings', as in 'dislike the sentimentality of the love songs' and 'She disliked her home town but now speaks about it with great sentimentality'.

separate, is frequently misspelt. Note the *a* following the *p*. It is a common error to put *e* in that position. As an adjective **separate** means 'forming a unit by itself, existing apart', as in 'occupy separate rooms' and 'lead separate lives'. It also means 'distinct, different', as in 'happening on five separate occasions' and 'separate problems'. As a verb **separate** means 'to divide', as in 'The roads separate further up'; 'to cause to divide', as in 'separate the group'; 'to keep apart', as in 'A river separates the two parts of the estate'; 'to stop living together', as in 'The child's parents have recently separated'.

sewed and **sewn** are interchangeable as the past participle of the verb 'to sew', as in 'She has sewed/sewn patches on the torn parts of the trousers'. When the participle is used as an adjective, **sewn** is the more common form, as in 'badly sewn seams'. **Sewed** is also the past tense of 'to sew', as in 'She sewed the garment by hand'.

sexism in language has been an issue for some time, and various attempts have been made to avoid it. For example, 'person' is often used where 'man' was traditionally used and 'he/she' substituted for 'he' in situations where the sex of the relevant person is unknown or unspecified.

ship *see* **boat**.

siege is frequently misspelt. Note the *ie* combination. It follows the '*i* before *e* except after *c*' rule, but it is a common error to put *ei* instead. **Siege** means 'the surrounding of a town, fortress, etc, in order to capture it'.

sine qua non is a Latin phrase that has been adopted into English and means 'essential condition, something that is absolutely necessary', as in 'It is a sine qua non of the agreement that the rent is paid on time'. It is used only in formal or legal contexts.

sitting room, living room, lounge and **drawing room** all refer to 'a room in a house used for relaxation and the receiving of guests'. Which word is used is largely a matter of choice. Some people object to the use of **lounge** as being pretentious but it is becoming increasingly common. **Drawing room** is a more formal word and applies to a room in rather a grand residence.

skilful, as in 'admire his skilful handling of the situation' is frequently misspelt. Note the single *l* before the *f*. In American English the word is spelt **skillful**.

slander *see* **libel**.

sometime and **some time** are liable to be confused. **Sometime** means 'at an unknown or unspecified time', as in

spelled

'We must get together sometime' and 'I saw her sometime last year'. There is a growing tendency in modern usage to spell this as **some time**. Originally **some time** was restricted to meaning 'a period of time', as in 'We need some time to think'.

spelled and **spelt** are both acceptable forms of the past tense and past participle of the verb 'to spell', as in 'They spelled/spelt the word wrongly' and 'He realized that he had spelled/spelt the word wrongly'.

spoiled and **spoilt** are both acceptable forms of the past tense and past participle of the verb 'to spoil', as in 'They spoiled/spoilt that child' and 'They have spoiled/spoilt that house with their renovations'. When the past participle is used adjectivally, **spoilt** is the usual form, as in 'a spoilt child'.

stadium causes problems with regard to its plural form. **Stadiums** and **stadia** are both acceptable. **Stadium** is derived from Latin and the original plural form followed the Latin and was **stadia.** However, anglicized plural forms are becoming more and more common in foreign words adopted into English, and **stadiums** is now becoming the more usual form.

stanch and **staunch** are both acceptable spellings of the word meaning 'to stop the flow of', as in 'stanch/staunch the blood from the wound in his head' and 'try to stanch/staunch the tide of violence'. **Staunch** also means 'loyal, firm', as in 'the team's staunch supporters'.

stank and **stunk** are liable to be confused. **Stank** and **stunk** can both act as the past tense of the verb 'to stink', as in ' The rotten cheese stank' and 'He stunk of stale beer'.

Stunk can also act as the past participle, as in 'This room has stunk of cigarette smoke for days'.

stationary and **stationery** are liable to be confused. They sound alike but have completely different meanings. **Stationary** means 'not moving, standing still', as in 'stationary vehicles'. **Stationery** refers to 'writing materials', as in 'office stationery'. An easy way to differentiate between them is to remember that **stationery** is bought from a 'stationer', which, like 'baker' and 'butcher', ends in -*er*.

staunch *see* **stanch**.

stimulant and **stimulus** are liable to be confused. Formerly the distinction between them was quite clear but now the distinction is becoming blurred. Traditionally **stimulant** refers to 'a substance, such as a drug, that makes a person more alert or more active', as in 'Caffeine is a stimulant'. **Stimulus** traditionally refers to 'something that rouses or encourages a person to action or greater effort', as in 'The promise of more money acted as a stimulus to the work force and they finished the job in record time'. In modern usage the words are beginning to be used interchangeably. In particular, **stimulus** is used in the sense of **stimulant** as well as being used in its own original sense.

storey and **story** are liable to be confused. They sound alike but have completely different meanings. **Storey** means 'level of a building, floor', as in 'a multi-storey car park' and 'They live on the second storey of the house'. **Story** means 'a tale', as in 'tell the children a bedtime story'. The plural of **storey** is **stories** and the

straight away

plural of **story** is **stories**. In American English, **story** is used for both meanings.

straight away and **straightaway** are both acceptable ways of spelling the expression for 'without delay, at once', as in 'attend to the matter straight away/straightaway'.

straitened and **straightened** are liable to be confused. They sound alike but have completely different meanings. **Straitened** means 'severely restricted' and is most commonly found in the phrase 'in straitened circumstances', which means 'in extremely difficult financial circumstances'. **Straightened** is the past tense and participle of the verb 'to straighten', as in 'They have straightened the road out' and 'with her straightened hair'.

strata *see* **stratum**.

stratagem and **strategy** are liable to be confused. They look and sound similar but they have different meanings. **Stratagem** means 'a scheme or trick', as in 'think of a stratagem to mislead the enemy' and 'devise a stratagem to gain entry to the building'. **Strategy** refers to 'the art of planning a campaign', as in 'generals meeting to put together a battle strategy', and 'a plan or policy, particularly a clever one, designed for a particular purpose', as in 'admire the strategy which he used to win the game'.

stratum and **strata** are liable to be confused. **Stratum** is the singular form and **strata** is the plural form of a word meaning 'a layer or level', as in 'a stratum of rock' and 'different strata of society'. It is a common error to use **strata** as a singular noun.

student *see* **pupil**.

subconscious and unconscious are used in different contexts. **Subconscious** means 'concerning those areas or activities of the mind of which one is not fully aware', as in 'a subconscious hatred of her parents' and 'a subconscious desire to hurt her sister'. **Unconscious** means 'unaware', as in 'She was unconscious of his presence' and 'unconscious of the damage which he had caused', and 'unintentional', as in 'unconscious humour' and 'an unconscious slight'. **Unconscious** also means 'having lost consciousness, insensible', as in 'knocked unconscious by the blow to his head'.

subjective *see* **objective**.

subsequent *see* **consequent**.

subsidence has two acceptable pronunciations. It can be pronounced either sub-*sid*-ens, with the emphasis on the middle syllable which rhymes with 'hide', or *sub*-sid-ens, with the emphasis on the first syllable and with the middle syllable rhyming with 'hid'. **Subsidence** means 'falling or sinking', as in 'the subsidence of houses in that street'.

such and **like** are liable to be confused. **Such** is used to introduce examples, as in 'herbs, such as chervil and parsley' and 'citrus fruits, such as oranges and lemons'. **Like** introduces comparisons. 'She hates horror films like *Silence of the Lambs*', and 'Very young children, like very old people, have to be kept warm.'

suit and **suite** are liable to be confused. They look similar but they have completely different meanings. **Suit** has several meanings. These include 'a set of clothes', as in 'He was wearing a tweed three-piece suit' (a jacket, trou-

237

sers and waistcoat in the same material) and 'She was married in a white suit, rather than a dress'; 'one of the four sets of playing cards', as in 'Which suit is trump?'; and 'an action in a court of law', as in 'bring a suit against her ex-husband for non-payment of maintenance'. **Suite** refers to 'a set of furniture', as in 'prefer non-matching chairs to the traditional three-piece suite' (a sofa and two armchairs in the same material); 'a set of rooms', as in 'book a suite at an expensive hotel' and 'the hotel's honeymoon suite'; and 'a musical composition consisting of three or more related parts', as in 'a ballet suite'. Note the *e* at the end of **suite**. **Suit** is pronounced *soot* or *syoot*. **Suite** is pronounced *sweet*.

supercilious is liable to be misspelt. Note the *c* and single *l*. It means 'condescending, disdainful', as in 'She treats unemployed people in a very supercilious way'.

supersede is frequently misspelt. Note the *-sede* ending. It is a common error to put *-cede* here, along the lines of 'precede'. **Supersede** means 'to take the place of, to replace', as in 'Word processors have superseded typewriters in many offices'.

supervise is frequently misspelt. Note the *-ise* ending. This is not one of the verbs that can be spelt ending in *-ize*. **Supervise** means 'to oversee', as in 'the teacher who was supervising the children in the playground' and 'a senior worker supervising the work of the trainees'.

supper *see* **dinner**.

susceptible is frequently misspelt. Note the *sc* combination and the *-ible*, not *-able*, ending. **Susceptible** means 'easily affected or influenced' and is frequently followed

by the preposition 'to', as in 'children who are susceptible to colds' and 'people who are susceptible to political
propaganda'.

swam and **swum** are not interchangeable. **Swam** is the
past tense of the verb 'to swim', as in 'They swam
ashore'. **Swum** is the past participle of the same verb, as
in 'The children have swum for long enough'.

swingeing and **swinging** are liable to be confused. They
look similar but they have completely different meanings. **Swinging** is simply the present participle of the
verb 'to swing', as in 'children swinging on the gate'. It
is also rather a dated term for 'lively and modern', as in
'the swinging sixties'. **Swingeing** means 'severe', as in
'swingeing cuts in public spending'. Note the *e* in
swingeing. Note also the pronunciation of **swingeing**. It
is pronounced *swin*-jing, not like swinging.

syndrome in its original meaning refers to 'a set of symp-
toms and signs that together indicate the presence of a
physical or mental disorder', as in 'Down's syndrome'.
In modern usage it is used loosely to indicate 'any set of
events, actions, characteristics, attitudes that together
make up, or are typical of, a situation', as in 'He suffers
from the "I'm all right Jack" syndrome and doesn't care
what happens to anyone else' and 'They seem to be caring people but they are opposing the building of an Aids
hospice in their street—a definite case of "the not in my
back yard" syndrome'.

T

target in its verb form, meaning 'to aim at', causes spelling problems with regard to its past participle, past tense and present participle. They are respectively **targeted** and **targeting**, as in 'resources targeted at the poorest section of the community' and 'the need for targeting their advertising campaign at young people.'

tariff is liable to be misspelt. Note the single *r* and double *f*. It means either 'duty to be paid on imported goods', as in 'the tariff payable on imported cars', or 'a list of fixed charges in a hotel, restaurant, etc', as in 'The hotel tariff is hanging behind the bedroom door' and 'the lunch tariff hanging outside the restaurant'.

tea *see* **dinner**.

teach *see* **learn**.

telephone *see* **phone**.

televise is frequently misspelt. Note the *-ise* ending. It is a common error to spell it with an *-ize* ending. It is helpful to remember the *s* of 'television'.

terminal and **terminus** in some contexts are interchangeable. They both refer to 'the end of a bus route, the last stop on a bus route, the building at the end of a bus route', as in 'The bus doesn't go any further—this is the terminus/terminal', but **terminus** is the more common term in this sense. They can also both mean 'the end of a rail-

way line, the station at the end of a railway line', but
terminal is the more common term in this sense. **Terminal** can refer to 'a building containing the arrival and
departure areas for passengers at an airport' and 'a building in the centre of a town for the arrival and departure
of air passengers'. **Terminal** also refers to 'a point of
connection in an electric circuit', as in 'the positive and
negative terminals', and 'apparatus, usually consisting
of a keyboard and screen, for communicating with the
central processor in a computing system', as in 'He has
a dumb terminal so he can read information but not input it'. As an adjective **terminal** means 'of, or relating
to, the last stage in a fatal illness', as in 'a terminal disease' and 'terminal patients'.

terminus *see* **terminal**.

tête-à-tête, meaning 'an intimate conversation between
two people', as in 'have a tête-à-tête with her best friends
about her marital problems', is liable to be misspelt. Note
the circumflex accent on the first *e* of each **tête** and the
accent on the *a*. The phrase has been adopted into English from French.

than is used to link two halves of comparisons or contrasts, as in 'Peter is considerably taller than John is',
'He is older than I am' and 'I am more informed about
the situation than I was yesterday'. Problems arise when
the relevant verb is omitted. In order to be grammatically correct, the word after 'than' should take the subject
form if there is an implied verb, as in 'He is older than I
(am)'. However this can sound stilted, as in 'She works
harder than he (does)', and in informal contexts this usu-

their

ally becomes 'She works harder than him'. If there is no implied verb, the word after **than** is in the object form, as in 'rather you than me!'

their and **there** are liable to be confused because they sound similar. **There** means 'in, to or at that place', as in 'place it there' and 'send it there'. **Their** is the possessive of 'they', meaning 'of them, belonging to them', as in 'their books' and 'their mistakes'.

their and **they're** are liable to be confused because they sound similar. **Their** is the possessive of 'they', meaning 'of them, belonging to them', as in 'their cars' and 'their attitudes'. **They're** is a shortened form of 'they are', as in 'They're not very happy' and 'They're bound to lose'.

they, used in conjunction with 'anyone', everyone', 'no one' and 'someone', is increasingly replacing 'he' or 'she', although to do so is ungrammatical. The reason for this is to avoid the sexism of using 'he' when the sex of the person being referred to is either unknown or unspecified, and to avoid the clumsiness of 'he/she' or 'he or she'. Examples of **they** being so used include 'Everyone must do their best' and 'No one is to take their work home'.

they're *see* **their**.

this *see* **next**.

threshold is liable to be misspelt. Note the single *h*. It is a common error to put double *h*. **Threshold** means either 'doorway', as in 'meet the other visitor on the threshold', or 'the beginning', as in 'on the threshold of a new career'.

till and **until** are more or less interchangeable except that
until is slightly more formal, as in 'They'll work till
they drop' and 'Until we assess the damage we will not
know how much the repairs will cost'.

tobacconist is frequently misspelt. Note the single *b*, the
double *c* and the single *n*. A **tobacconist** refers to 'a person or shop that sells tobacco, cigarettes and cigars'.

toilet, **lavatory**, **loo** and **bathroom** all have the same meaning but the context in which they are used sometimes
varies. **Toilet** is the most widely used of the words and
is used on signs in public places. The informal **loo** is also
very widely used. **Lavatory** is less common nowadays
although it was formerly regarded by all but the working class and lower-middle class as the most acceptable
term. **Bathroom** in British English usually refers to 'a
room containing a bath', but in American English it is
the usual word for **toilet**. **Ladies** and **gents** are terms for
toilet, particularly in public places. **Powder room** also
means this, as does the American English **rest room**.

town *see* **city**.

trade names should be written with a capital letter, as in
'Filofax' and 'Jacuzzi'. When trade names are used as
verbs they are written with a lower case letter, as in 'hoover the carpet'.

trafficker is frequently misspelt. Note the *k*. The word
means 'a person who deals in or trades in something,
particularly something illegal or dishonest', as in 'drugs
traffickers'. Note also **trafficked** and **trafficking** but
traffic.

trait is traditionally pronounced *tray* but *trayt* is also an acceptable pronunciation in modern usage. It means an element or quality in someone's personality', as in 'One of his least attractive traits is his habit of blaming other people for his mistakes'.

tranquillity, meaning 'peace, peaceful state', as in 'disturb the tranquillity of the countryside', is liable to be misspelt. Note the double *l*.

travel causes problems with regard to the past participle, past tense and present participle. The *l* doubles before '-ed' and '-ing' are added, as **travelled** and **travelling**, as in 'They travelled to many parts of the world' and 'nervous when travelling by car'. Note also **traveller**, as in 'travellers in foreign lands'. In American English the *l* is not doubled, as **traveled, traveling** and **traveler**.

troop and **troupe** are liable to be confused. **Troop** refers to 'a military unit', as in 'the officer in charge of the troop', or to 'a group or collection of people or animals', as in 'Troops of people arrived at the demonstration from all over the country'. **Troupe** refers to 'a company of actors or performers', as in 'a troupe of acrobats'.

try to and **try and** are interchangeable in modern usage. Formerly **try and** was considered suitable only in spoken and very informal contexts, but it is now considered acceptable in all but the most formal contexts, as in 'Try to/and do better' and 'They must try to/and put the past behind them'.

twelfth, as in 'December is the twelfth month of the year', is liable to be both mispronounced and misspelt. The *f* is frequently omitted in error in pronunciation and spelling.

U

ultra is used as a prefix meaning 'going beyond', as in 'ultraviolet' and 'ultrasound', or 'extreme, very', as in 'ultra-sophisticated', ultra-modern, and 'ultra-conservative'. Compounds using it may be spelt with or without a hyphen. Words such as 'ultrasound' and 'ultraviolet' are usually spelt as one word, but words with the second sense of **ultra**, such as 'ultra-sophisticated', are often hyphenated.

unaware and **unawares** are not interchangeable. **Unaware** is an adjective meaning 'not aware, not conscious of', as in 'He was unaware that he was being watched' and 'She was unaware of his presence', and 'ignorant, having no knowledge of', as in 'politically unaware'. **Unawares** is an adverb meaning 'without being aware, without noticing, unintentionally', as in 'I must have dropped my keys unawares' and 'The child dropped her gloves unawares', or 'by surprise, unexpected, without warning', as in 'The enemy attack took them unawares' and 'The snowstorm caught the climbers unawares'.

unconscious *see* **subconscious**.

underhand and **underhanded** are interchangeable in the sense of 'sly, deceitful', as in 'He used underhand/underhanded methods to get the job' and 'It was under-

245

hand/underhanded of him to not to tell her that he was leaving'. **Underhand** is the more common of the two terms.

under way, meaning 'in progress', is traditionally spelt as two words, as in 'Preparations for the conference are under way'. In modern usage it is frequently spelt as one word, as in 'The expansion project is now underway'. It is a common error to write 'under weigh'.

undoubtedly, as in 'He is undoubtedly the best player in the team' and 'Undoubtedly we shall be a little late', is liable to be misspelt. A common error is to spell it 'Undoubtably', probably in confusion with 'indubitably'. **Undoubtedly** means the same as 'without a doubt'.

unexceptionable and **unexceptional** are liable to be confused. They look and sound rather similar but they have different meanings. **Unexceptionable** means 'not liable to be criticized or objected to, inoffensive, satisfactory', as in 'His behaviour was quite unexceptionable' and 'I found her remarks quite unexceptionable'. **Unexceptional** means 'ordinary, not outstanding or unusual', as in 'She was supposed to be a brilliant player but her performance was unexceptional' and 'an unexceptional student'.

uninterested *see* **disinterested**.

unique traditionally means 'being the only one of its kind', as in 'a unique work of art' and 'everyone's fingerprints are unique' and so cannot be modified by such words as 'very', 'rather', 'more', etc, although it can be modified by 'almost' and 'nearly'. In modern usage **unique** is often used to mean 'unrivalled, unparalleled, outstand-

ing', as in 'a unique opportunity' and 'a unique performance'.

unreadable *see* **illegible.**

unrepairable *see* **irreparable.**

until *see* **till.**

unwanted and **unwonted** are liable to be confused. They
sound alike but they have completely different meanings. **Unwanted** means 'not wanted', as in 'give unwanted furniture to a charity shop', 'an unwanted pregnan-
cy' and 'feel unwanted'. **Unwonted** means 'not custom-
ary, not usual', as in 'behave with unwonted courtesy'
and 'a feeling of unwonted optimism'. **Unwonted** is not
pronounced in the same way as **unwanted**. It is pronounced un-*wont*-ed with the second syllable pronounced
as 'won't'.

up and **upon** mean the same and are virtually interchangeable, except that **upon** is slightly more formal. Examples include 'sitting on a bench', 'the carpet on the floor',
'the stamp on the letter', caught with the stolen goods
on him' and 'something on his mind'; and 'She threw
herself upon her dying mother's bed', 'a carpet of snow
upon the ground' and 'Upon his arrival he went straight
upstairs'.

upward and **upwards** are not interchangeable. **Upward**
is used as an adjective, as in 'on an upward slope' and
'an upward trend in prices'. **Upwards** is an adverb, as in
'look upwards to see the plane'.

urban and **urbane** are liable to be confused. They look
similar but they have completely different meanings.
Urban means 'of a town or city', as in 'urban dwellers'

usable

and 'in an urban setting'. **Urbane** means 'smoothly elegant and sophisticated', as in 'an urbane wit' and 'an urbane man of the world'.

usable and **useable** are both acceptable spellings, as in 'furniture which is no longer usable/useable' and 'crockery which is scarcely usable/useable'. **Usable** is more common.

V

vacation, meaning 'holiday', in British English is mostly restricted to a university or college situation, as in 'students seeking paid employment during their vacation'. In American English it is the usual word for 'holiday'.

vaccinate is liable to be misspelt. Note the double *c* and single *n*. The word means 'to inject a vaccine into to prevent a particular disease', as in 'vaccinate the children against tuberculosis'. **Vaccine** refers to 'a substance that is injected into the bloodstream and protects the body against a disease by making it have a mild form of the disease', as in 'a vaccine against smallpox'.

vacuum is liable to be misspelt. Note the single *c* and double *u*. It refers to 'a space that is completely empty of all matter and gases', as in 'create a total vacuum'.

variegated is liable to be misspelt. Note the *e* between the *i* and the *g*. It means 'varied in colour, speckled or mottled with different colours', as in 'variegated leaves'. It is pronounced *vayr*-i-gayt-ed.

verbal and **oral** are liable to be confused. **Oral** means 'expressed in speech', as in 'an oral, rather than a written examination'. **Verbal** means 'expressed in words', as in 'He asked for an instruction diagram but he was given verbal instructions' and 'They were going to stage a protest match but they settled for a verbal protest'. It is also used to mean 'referring to the spoken word, expressed in speech', as in 'a verbal agreement'. Because of these two possible meanings, the use of **verbal** can lead to ambiguity. In order to clarify the situation, **oral** should be used when 'expressed in speech' is meant. **Verbal** can also mean referring to verbs, as in 'verbal endings'. For more information on **oral** *see* **aural**.

vice versa means 'the other way round, with the order reversed', as in 'He will do his friend's shift and vice versa' and 'Mary dislikes John and vice versa'. It is pronounced vis-e ver-sa, vi-si ver-sa or vis ver-sa and is derived from Latin.

vigorous is liable to be misspelt. Note the absence of *u* before *r*, unlike the noun **vigour**. It means 'strong and energetic', as in 'vigorous young men playing football', or 'forceful', as in 'vigorous debate' and 'vigorous criticism'.

vis-à-vis means 'in relation to', as in 'their performance vis-à-vis their ability' and 'the company's policy vis-à-vis early retirement'. It is pronounced vee-za-vee and is derived from French. Note the accent on the *a*.

vitamin is pronounced vit-a-min, with the first syllable rhyming with 'lit' in British English. In American English the first syllable rhymes with 'light'. The word refers to 'one of a group of substances which are essential for healthy life, different ones occurring in different foods', as in a 'sufferer from a deficiency of vitamin B6' and 'Citrus fruits are a source of vitamin C'.

victuals, meaning 'food', as in 'children requiring nourishing victuals', is liable to be mispronounced. It is pronounced vitlz.

W

-ways *see* **-wise**.

weaved, wove and **woven** can cause problems. **Wove** is
the usual past tense of the verb 'to weave', as in 'She
wove the cloth on a hand loom', 'The spider wove a
web' and 'The children wove a garland of flowers'.
However, in the sense of 'to move along by twisting and
turning' **weaved** is the past tense, as in 'The cyclist
weaved in and out of the traffic' and 'The drunks weaved
their way home'. **Woven** is the past participle of all but
'the twisting and turning' sense, as in 'She had woven
the cloth herself' and 'The children had woven garlands'.
Weaved is the past participle, as in 'She has weaved her
way through the traffic'.

weird is liable to be misspelt. Note the *ei* combination.
The word means 'strange, uncanny, unnatural', as in 'see
weird figures in the mist' and 'hear weird cries in the
night'. It also means 'unusual, bizarre, unconventional',
as in 'wear weird clothes' and 'have a weird sense of
humour'.

wet and **whet** are liable to be confused. **Wet** means 'to
cover with moisture', as in 'Wet the clay before using it'
and 'wet one's lips'. **Whet** means 'to sharpen', as in
'whet the blade of the sword', and 'to stimulate, excite',
as in 'whet his appetite for adventure'.

what ever

what ever and **whatever** are not interchangeable. **What ever** is used when 'ever' is used for emphasis, as in 'What ever does he think he's doing?' and 'What ever is she wearing'. **Whatever** means 'anything, regardless of what, no matter what', as in 'Help yourself to whatever you want' and 'Whatever he says I don't believe him'.

whet *see* **wet**.

which and **what** can cause problems. In questions **which** is used when a limited range of alternatives is suggested, as in 'Which book did you buy in the end?' and **what** is used in general situations, as in 'What book did you buy?'

whisky and **whiskey** both refer to a strong alcoholic drink distilled from grain. **Whisky** is made in Scotland and **whiskey** in Ireland and America. **Whisky** is the usual British English spelling.

who and **whom** cause problems. **Who** is the subject of a verb, as in 'Who told you?', 'It was you who told her' and 'the girls who took part in the play'. **Whom** is the object of a verb or preposition, as in 'Whom did he tell?', 'To whom did you speak?' and 'the people from whom he stole'. In modern usage **whom** is falling into disuse, especially in questions, except in formal contexts. **Who** is used instead even although it is ungrammatical, as in 'Who did you speak to?' **Whom** should be retained when it is a relative pronoun, as in 'the man whom you saw', 'the person to whom he spoke' and 'the girl to whom she gave the book'.

whose and **who's** are liable to be confused. They sound alike but have different meanings. **Whose** means 'of whom' or 'of which', as in 'the woman whose child won', 'the boy whose leg was broken', 'Whose bicycle is that?' and 'the firm whose staff went on strike'. **Who's** is a shortened form of 'who is', as in 'Who's that?', 'Who's first in the queue?' and 'Who's coming to the cinema?'

wilful is liable to be misspelt. Note the single *l* before *f*, and the final single *l*. It means 'done deliberately, unintentional', as in 'wilful damage done to the phone box', or 'headstrong, obstinate', as in 'a wilful child'. In American English the word is spelt with a double *l*, as 'willful'.

-wise and **-ways** cause problems. Added to nouns, **-wise** can form adverbs of manner indicating either 'in such a position or direction', as in 'lengthwise' and 'clockwise', and 'in the manner of', as in 'crabwise'. In modern usage **-wise** is frequently used to mean 'with reference to', as in 'Weatherwise it was fine', 'Workwise all is well' and 'Moneywise they're not doing too well'. The suffix **-ways** has a more limited use. It means 'in such a way, direction or manner of', as in 'lengthways' and 'sideways'.

withhold is sometimes misspelt. Note the double *h*. It means 'to keep back', as in 'withhold evidence'.

woman *see* **lady**.

worship causes problems with regard to the past tense, past participle and present participle as **worshipped, worshipping**. Note also **worshipper** but **worshipful**.

wove *see* **weaved**.

wrack *see* **rack**.

X

Xerox causes problems with regard to both spelling and pronunciation. It is a registered trademark for 'a type of photographic process used for copying documents, etc', as in 'a Xerox photocopier', or 'a copy made using this process', as in 'a Xerox of the contract'. Since it is a registered trademark the noun must be spelt with a capital letter. **Xerox** can also be a verb meaning 'to copy a document using the Xerox process' and can be spelt with either a capital letter or a lower-case letter, as in 'Please Xerox/xerox these letters before posting them'.

Xmas is sometimes used as an alternative and shorter form of 'Christmas'. It is common only in a written informal context and is used mainly in commercial situations, as in 'Xmas cards on sale here' and 'Get your Xmas tree here'. When pronounced it is the same as 'Christmas'. The X derives from the Greek *chi*, the first letter of *Christos*, the Greek word for Christ.

X-ray is usually written with an initial capital letter when it is a noun meaning 'a photograph made by means of X-rays showing the bones or organs of the body', as in 'take an X-ray of the patient's chest'. Another term for the noun **X-ray** is 'radiograph'. As a verb it is also usually spelt with an initial capital, as 'After the accident he had his leg X-rayed', but it is sometimes spelt with an initial lower-case letter, as in 'have his chest x-rayed'.

Y

yoghurt is the most usual spelling of the word for 'a type of semi-liquid consisting of milk fermented by added bacteria', as in 'have yoghurt and fruit for breakfast', but **yogurt** and **yoghourt** are also acceptable spellings. It is usually pronounced yog-ert, but yoh-gert is also a possible pronunciation and is the standard one in American English.

yoke and **yolk** are liable to be confused. They sound alike but have completely different meanings. **Yolk**, referring to 'the yellow part of an egg', as in 'The yolk of this egg is too soft', is the commoner of the two words. **Yoke** has several meanings. It means 'a connecting bar', as in 'the yoke across the necks of the oxen' and 'a peasant carrying two pails of water on a yoke'; 'a pair of oxen', as in 'owning three yoke of oxen'; 'an oppressive control', as in 'under the yoke of the cruel tyrant'; 'the part of a garment fitting round the shoulders or hips from which the rest of the garment hangs', as in 'a sweater with a contrasting-coloured yolk'. Both words are pronounced yok to rhyme with 'poke'.

you is used in informal or less formal situations to indicate an indefinite person referred to as 'one' in formal situations. Examples include 'You learn a foreign language more quickly if you spend some time in the country where it is spoken', 'You would think that they would

your

make sure that their staff are polite', 'You can get used to anything in time' and 'You have to experience the situation to believe it'. **You** in this sense must be distinguished from **you** meaning the second person singular', as in 'You have missed your bus', 'You must know where you left your bag' and 'You have to leave now'. *See* **one**.

your and **you're** are liable to be confused. **Your** is a possessive adjective meaning 'belonging to you, of you', as in 'That is your book and this is mine', 'Your attitude is surprising' and 'It is your own fault'. **You're** is a shortened form of 'you are', as in 'You're foolish to believe him', 'You're going to be sorry' and 'You're sure to do well. Note the spelling of the pronoun **yours**, as in 'This book is yours' and 'Which car is yours?' It should not be spelt with an apostrophe as it is not a shortened form of anything.

yours *see* **your**.

yuppie *see* **acronyms**.